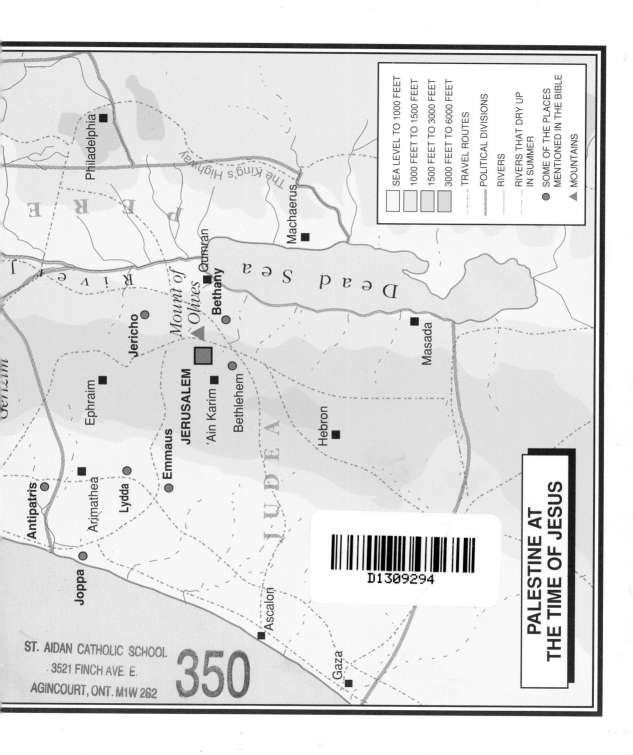

PALESTINE AT
THE TIME OF JESUS

SEA LEVEL TO 1000 FEET
1000 FEET TO 1500 FEET
1500 FEET TO 3000 FEET
3000 FEET TO 6000 FEET
TRAVEL ROUTES
POLITICAL DIVISIONS
RIVERS
RIVERS THAT DRY UP
IN SUMMER
SOME OF THE PLACES
MENTIONED IN THE BIBLE
MOUNTAINS

The King's Highway

Philadelphia

P   E   R   E

Machaerus

Dead Sea

Qumran

Mount of Olives

Bethany

Jericho

Masada

Ephraim

JERUSALEM

'Ain Karim

Bethlehem

Hebron

Emmaus

Gerizim

Antipatris

Arimathea

Lydda

J   U   D   E   A

Joppa

Ascalon

Gaza

29

Year 4

Come
and See

English Canadian Catechetical Series

CCCB

BORN *of* **THE SPIRIT**

CANADIAN CATECHETICAL PROGRAM

Contents

 Canadian Conference of Catholic Bishops
Conférence des évêques catholiques du Canada

Dear Boys and Girls,

You love a good story: a story of discovery, a story that is true and especially one that involves you.

Come and See is an invitation for you to get to know Jesus in a personal way, to develop your friendship with him, and to become involved in his work of bringing people into the circle of God's love.

This program has been designed especially for you. This year you will discover how the story of Jesus has been handed on to us over a space of 2000 years:
- through the written Word of God (Bible);
- through the constant retelling and reflection on his life and teaching (Tradition);
- through our celebration of the major events and actions of his life (Liturgy);
- and through the influence and example of people whose lives reflect the goodness and love of Jesus (Spirituality).

May you come to know and love the Lord Jesus and become part of his on-going story. May Jesus become a very important part of your life story, too!

Yours sincerely in Christ,

+ Peter J. Mallon

Peter J. Mallon
Archbishop of Regina

Unit 1
The Church hands on the good news

Theme 1 New beginnings
Theme 2 The Church hands on the story of Jesus
Theme 3 We explore the New Testament

1 New beginnings

Hi! My name is Natash
Here are the secrets of
my code!

What's your class story?
Do you remember your
friends' secret codes?

**With your friends, make a
list in your Big Book of
Remembering of all that
you remember.**

Breadmaking

The magic hour had come. Everyone was there and the house was filled with excitement. Aunts, uncles, and cousins – they had all come to celebrate the day. Laughter echoed in the dining room as the family gathered around the huge oak table for the morning meal. Suddenly, the kitchen door burst open and the hot, golden bread was carried high to Mario's place at the head of the table. The room blushed with hugs and handshakes and kisses, then fell to a hush as all eyes turned to the young boy who had made this special day come true.

"We're a family!" he said as he took one of the golden loaves. He felt a joy inside him that was like a river flowing out of a dry land. He wanted to sing and dance and twirl about for the sheer energy inside him. Then, for a moment, he just wanted to hold the bread and remember how they had made it. Together.

Not so long ago, they had gone shopping among walls of green cucumbers and soft, red tomatoes. She taught him all the little things, like how to shop, how to buy food and bring it home. And she had taught him to call her Nonna because that was the way they said "Grandma" in the Old Country. He was Mario. She was Nonna. And they were best friends. Nonna was big on the Old Country. In the evening, when the sun hung low and orange in the sky, Mario liked to perch on Nonna's fluffy feather bed to hear stories of long, long ago. Mario thought that Nonna was the best storyteller in the whole world, and he rested his head on the soft hump of her knees. This was their dream-time together, when grandfathers and great-grandfathers came alive and joked and laughed and did wonderful things.

Every day they were together, Mario and Nonna. They laughed when things were light and happy. They cried when things were heavy and sad. But their favourite time, more than all the other times, was their baking time, when they got together in the warm, cozy kitchen to make Easter bread. That was special, and Nonna taught him all the things he needed to know.

"Be careful you don't crack the eggs, Mario," she said. "If they crack they're no good to put in the little nest of Easter bread. Our 'pane di pasqua' – that's what we call it in Italian." And the brightly coloured eggs glistened in the water, waiting to take their place of honour on the top of the soft bread.

"Do you make it just for Easter?" Mario asked.

"No, for special breakfasts, too. We could make it for your First Communion. I remember we had it in the Old Country, when your father was baptized, and when your grandfather and I were coming to this country." Then Nonna started to talk about that other time, when Mario's grandfather and father and Nonna had first come here, and how lonely and strange they had felt in the new land. But they had stayed together, and worked and learned and laughed. "We were a family then, Mario!"

Mario thought a long time about their coming to this country. It was as if the new land had made them a promise, and so they had stayed.

On Good Friday, Mario made his promise to Nonna. They were baking bread together. He watched as her strong fingers pressed deep into the dough. When she became tired, he slipped in to take her place. "You remind me of your father when he was your age," she said. "He used to help me, too, you know. But then he got big, went away and forgot about our family customs. No time to help his mother in the kitchen." Mario knew she was sad about that.

"Don't you forget, Mario," she said.

He looked up. "I won't, Nonna. I promise."

You could tell that he meant forever. The promise was like gold!

What was the promise?

How did Mario and Nonna keep it?

How was it like gold?

We are a family!

What gathering times do you treasure with your family?

Why are these times special?

Decorate the cover of your remembering book with favourite family events.

The story of Pentecost

Pentecost – the beginning of the Church!

The friends of Jesus were "filled with the Holy Spirit" (Acts 2.4). The Spirit changed them so that they weren't afraid anymore. They learned something so important that they became like new people. What they learned was about Jesus. The Holy Spirit taught them that Jesus was not dead – he was with God, and that "God has made this Jesus... both Lord and Christ" (Acts 2.36). Jesus' words and actions were true. He became the most important figure in their lives. The disciples proclaimed this good news far and wide. The Holy Spirit helped Peter speak so that many believed that day. The Holy Spirit helped the disciples tell people what God had done in the person of Jesus. This was the beginning of the Church.

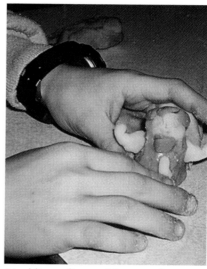

Moulding a figure of Jesus in clay.

Share the story of Pentecost at home. Tell why Pentecost happened. Draw a picture to go with the story.

**Give thanks to the Holy Spirit for new beginnings.
Pray the Holy Spirit prayer together:**

Come, Holy Spirit

V. Come, Holy Spirit, fill the hearts of your faithful.
R. And kindle in them the fire of your love.
V. Send forth your Spirit and they shall be created.
R. And you will renew the face of the earth.

Let us pray.
Lord,
by the light of the Holy Spirit,
you have taught the hearts of your faithful.
In the same Spirit
help us to relish what is right
and always rejoice in your consolation.
We ask this through Christ our Lord. Amen.

A Book of Prayers (ICEL)

Remember

The Holy Spirit came on the day of Pentecost to help the disciples tell the story of Jesus. On Pentecost Sunday we celebrate the birth of the Church.

2 The Church hands on the story of Jesus

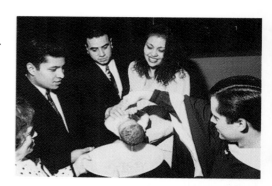

Tradition:
Where are we coming from?
What traditions are being
handed on in these photographs?
Why do you think people want to
preserve their traditions?

What do our traditions tell us about who we are
- as a family?
- as a community?
- as Church?

Sometimes, when great buildings are built, people make a collection of things and seal them into a wall as a "time capsule." That way, people of the future will know more about the history of the building and the people who made it.

If you were making a time capsule for your family, what would you collect?

Create a time capsule with your family.
Decide on what you would like to hand on.
Draw pictures, write stories or letters, add mementoes and put them all into a container of your choice. Share the contents with your friends!

An ancient time capsule!

One winter day in 1947, a young Bedouin boy named Muhammad was tending his goats on the hillside close to the Dead Sea. When he saw that one of his goats was missing, he went off to search for it. Climbing back up the hill, he came to the entrance of a cave and threw a stone inside. He heard something break. It was an earthen jar. Inside was a leather scroll. Experts said it was about 2000 years old! Because of the dry air in the cave, the scroll had been very well preserved.

Facts and figures!

- At first no one was interested in the scrolls, but Muhammed finally sold them to a merchant from Bethlehem, who then sold them to a bishop in Jerusalem.

- When they finally reached the archaeologists, there was great excitement; they found that the scrolls could be dated between 20 B.C.E. and 70 C.E. They were almost 2000 years old!

More on the next page 👉

Archaeologists were soon swarming over the hillsides to explore the other caves. Between 1947 and 1956, they searched 200 caves and found about 600 ancient scrolls and fragments. There were manuscripts from almost every book of the Old Testament. Then Bible scholars slowly and patiently began putting them together, like the pieces of a giant jigsaw puzzle. The Dead Sea scrolls are priceless treasures. They tell a most remarkable story.

To whom did the scrolls belong?

Why were they hidden in the caves?

What did Muhammad do with the scrolls?

Why do you think these scrolls are such great treasures?

Do you know what we call them?

◄ Jars from Qumran in which some of the Dead Sea scrolls were found.

- Between 1947 and 1956, 200 caves were searched and about 600 ancient scrolls or fragments were found.

- The scrolls had belonged to a library of a Jewish community of monks known as Essenes in Qumran.

- When the Roman army invaded Palestine in 68 C.E., the monks quickly packed away their precious treasures and hid them in the natural caves behind their monastery.

- These scrolls contained entire pages from all the books of the Old Testament except the Book of Esther.

- The care these Essenes took as they copied these texts and hid them shows how important the books of the Bible were to this community.

- Today, the Dead Sea scrolls are kept in a beautiful building called the Shrine of the Book, which is part of the Israel Museum in Jerusalem.

- Search for the Dead Sea scrolls on the Internet!

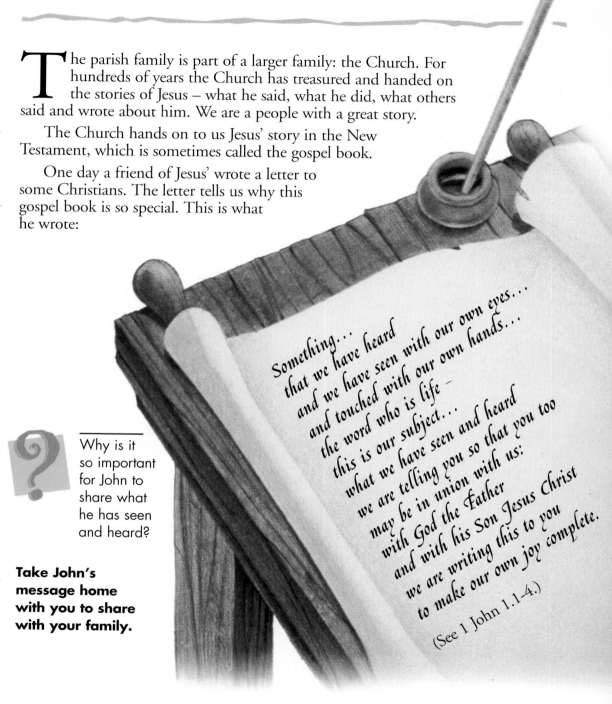

The parish family is part of a larger family: the Church. For hundreds of years the Church has treasured and handed on the stories of Jesus – what he said, what he did, what others said and wrote about him. We are a people with a great story.

The Church hands on to us Jesus' story in the New Testament, which is sometimes called the gospel book.

One day a friend of Jesus' wrote a letter to some Christians. The letter tells us why this gospel book is so special. This is what he wrote:

Why is it so important for John to share what he has seen and heard?

Take John's message home with you to share with your family.

Something...
that we have heard
and we have seen with our own eyes...
and touched with our own hands –
the word who is life –
this is our subject...
what we have seen and heard
we are telling you so that you too
may be in union with us:
with God the Father
and with his Son Jesus Christ
we are writing this to you
to make our own joy complete.

(See 1 John 1.1-4.)

Opening prayer

We praise you, loving God,
for your Word Jesus Christ.
Give us your Holy Spirit
to listen to your Word with our ears,
to treasure it with our hearts
and to live it with our lives.
This we ask through your Word
  Jesus Christ
who lives and reigns with you
in the unity of the Holy Spirit
one God for ever and ever. Amen.

Word of God

Something...
that we have heard
and we have seen with
  our own eyes...
and touched with our
  own hands;
the Word who is life –
this is our subject...

Ritual action

"Elizabeth, receive from the Church
  the good news of Jesus Christ.
May it touch your mind, your lips
  and your heart."

For the Church, who treasures and
  hands on to us the good news of Jesus.
We thank you, God.

18

Closing

Through the gift of your
*   Spirit, loving God,*
the early followers of Jesus
proclaimed the joy of
*   the good news*
to people everywhere.
Give us that same joy
and help us to share it
*   with all people.*
We ask this through Jesus Christ
who lives and reigns with you
in the unity of the Holy Spirit
one God for ever and ever. Amen.

new words

tradition: the handing on of customs, beliefs and practices from generation to generation.

archaeologists: Men and women who try to find out about people who lived long ago by studying what these people left behind – like buildings, tools and dishes.

Remember

From its very beginning, the Church has handed on the good news of Jesus Christ.

3 We explore the New Testament

How did you feel about the celebration of good news?

How did you gather? Who was there? What did you see?

What did you hear? How was God's Word proclaimed?

How did you feel when the Book of God's Word was placed in your hands? What does this tell you about the Church? about God?

How did you go forth?

Draw a picture of the celebration in your remembering book to share at home.

Do you know where your stump came from? What kind of tree was it?

How did you feel when you saw your tree stories and pictures around the Book of God's Word? What does this tell you about God's Word?

With your friends, plan a trip to find a story tree for the year. Examine the tree carefully – what it looks like in fall, what it sounds like when you put your ear against its trunk or how it feels when you rub your hand against its bark. Carry its memory back to class with you. Draw pictures of the tree and put them together to create a backdrop for your gathering space. The colourful backdrop will remind us of the stump and the life that it holds: the living word of God that rests upon it. Bring back favourite fall leaves to sprinkle around, too.

When fall turns to winter, visit the tree again. And in springtime. As the seasons turn, bring each memory back to fill your gathering space with living colour.

To Catholics of the Byzantine–Ukrainian Church, the gospel book is precious. Here are some of the ways that the Byzantine–Ukrainian community shows reverence for God's word:

- The gospel book is beautifully decorated.
- It is always kept on the altar.
- The priest kisses the gospel book when he first comes to the altar.
- Short acclamations are sung before the word is read.
- The book is incensed to show reverence to Christ, present in his word.

Look at the gospel book cover. What do you see? What does it mean? How do Catholics of the Roman Church show reverence for the Bible?

The Bible is the most precious of all our books. We sometimes call it the "Book of God's Word."

Although the Bible is just one book, it is like a library of books!

It is divided into two parts: the Old Testament and the New Testament. The Old Testament tells the story of God's love for the Jewish people. The New Testament continues God's story of love. It is about the life of Jesus and his message of the kingdom.

The New Testament contains 27 books!

Use the New Testament collection to help you find all 27 books. Decide where to fit them in the columns below.

Gospels	Acts of the Apostles	21 Letters	Revelation
The story of the good news of Jesus according to: • Matthew • Mark • Luke • John	Luke's story of the friends of Jesus after his death and resurrection	Letters written by followers of Jesus to different people and Churches	A book written to give hope to Christians that Jesus will give life even when things are very hard

There are different translations of the Bible. Look at your translation. What version do you have? Jerusalem Bible? Revised Standard Version?

We sometimes call the New Testament our gospel book. Do you know what the word "gospel" means? Check it out on the next page.

This year you will explore the good news and discover more about the story of Jesus using the four gospel accounts of Matthew, Mark, Luke and John. Matthew, Mark, Luke and John are called "evangelists." Check out what this word means on the next page.

THE BIBLE

THE LAW
Genesis · Exodus · Leviticus · Numbers · Deuteronomy

THE PROPHETS
Joshua · Judges · I Samuel · II Samuel · I Kings · II Kings · Isaiah · Jeremiah · Ezekiel · Hosea · Joel · Amos · Obadiah · Jonah · Micah · Nahum · Habakkuk · Zephaniah · Haggai · Zechariah · Malachi

WRITINGS
Psalms · Proverbs · Job · Daniel · Ezra · Nehemiah · I Chronicles · II Chronicles · Song of Songs · Ruth · Lamentations · Ecclesiastes · Esther · Tobit · Judith · Wisdom · Sirach · Baruch · I Maccabees · II Maccabees

THE GOSPELS
Matthew · Mark · Luke · John

THE ACTS OF THE APOSTLES
Acts

LETTERS
Romans · I Corinthians · II Corinthians · Galatians · Ephesians · Philippians · Colossians · I Thessalonians · II Thessalonians · I Timothy · II Timothy · Titus · Philemon · Hebrews · James · I Peter · II Peter · I John · II John · III John · Jude

REVELATION
Revelation

Finding your way around the Bible

Each book of the Bible is divided into chapters. A chapter is divided into verses. (A verse is usually one or two sentences.) Verses are marked with smaller numbers. The name of the book is always at the top of each page.

If you look closely at the picture on this page, you will see that it is the story of your good friend Zacchaeus. Now, pick up your Bible and find Luke 19.1 and the story of Zacchaeus for yourself! (Clue: Find the table of contents at the beginning of the Bible to get the page number for Luke's gospel.)

When we see Luke 19.1-10, we read it this way: "The Gospel according to Luke, chapter 19, verses 1 to 10."

How would you read these?

- Matthew 13.31-32
- John 14.1
- Mark 10.13-14

Get together with a friend. Take turns finding the references below in your bibles:

- Matthew 13.31-32
- Matthew 7.12
- Matthew 9.9
- Mark 4.30-32
- Mark 4.38
- Mark 15.17
- Luke 2.11
- Luke 14.21-22
- Luke 19.5-6
- John 6.29
- John 21.25
- John 7.12

new words

Bible: comes from the Greek words *ta Biblia*, which means "the books."

gospel: comes from an old English word, god-spel, which means "good news."

evangelist: a messenger of the good news.

Remember

The New Testament contains four gospels: the Gospel according to Matthew, Mark, Luke and John. Gospel means "good news" – the good news of Jesus Christ.

Unit 2
The good news about Jesus Christ

Theme 4 The Holy Spirit helps the disciples to remember Jesus
Theme 5 First memories of Jesus: the call to "Come and see"
Theme 6 And great crowds followed Jesus

4 The Holy Spirit helps the disciples to remember Jesus

Memories last forever

November came and went, came and went, came and went – all three times and not a word was spoken. Everything seemed so dead and silent in November. It was very strange. It used to be so different. The first snowflakes always fell in November and we would run excitedly to the old winter trunk to dig out our mittens and scarves. The stars came out earlier and earlier in November. And the big Advent wreath at church announced again and again that Christmas was just around the corner. November used to be filled with excitement, used to be worth waiting for. But not anymore. Not since the big snowstorm.

It was four years since the tragedy. It had started out as a beautiful fall day. Soon that all changed. The snow and sleet came quickly. My big brother Jaz lost control of his jeep on a turn and skidded off the road. He died instantly. Our family died that day, too.

We were a festive family. Occasions were fun times. We would even celebrate my cat's birthday. Jaz would play "Happy Birthday" for Bingo on his flute. Now special times were solemn, filled with awkward moments. Something was wrong and I didn't know how to fix it.

Christmas number four came and I had an idea. After dinner I said, "I have something for all of us to hear." I gently laid the flute on the table. I pressed the play button on the tape recorder. The room filled with the beautiful sound of music. It was Jaz's favourite and he always played it for us. It was like old times again.

My mother tried to hide the tears. My younger brother said, "I miss him so." Dad said, "He brought us together." We talked long into the evening. Jaz was back with us again. "Do you remember how he got the name 'Jaz'?" Mom asked. Joey said, "Tell us," even though he knew the story well. She laughed and told how Jaz had always loved music. He carried his toy flute with him from the time he was a toddler. Once, during one of his pretend performances, Grandpa called him Jaz. The name fit and it stuck like glue.

My idea had worked! There were so many, many memories. We were able to include Jaz in our family again. The big hurt was still in our hearts but the fun memories warmed our house. Now we were free to cherish them openly and carry him with us forever.

Why do you think the family wouldn't talk about Jaz?

How do you think they were all feeling?

What happened after they started to talk about Jaz?

How did the death of Jaz make his family see him?

What can we learn from our memories?

How is this story like the story "Breadmaking"?

Draw a picture of the story in your remembering book. Share it at home.

In a book of the Bible called the Acts of the Apostles, St. Luke tells us how the friends of Jesus lived after Pentecost. They remembered what Jesus had taught and how Jesus had lived, and they wanted to be like him.

Luke tells us that these first Christians were FAITHFUL to Jesus. This means they were full of faith. They really believed that Jesus was alive and that his Spirit was with them, changing their hearts and helping them to love like Jesus. Luke says that they were FAITHFUL in many ways.

• They were faithful to LOVING ONE ANOTHER.

• They were faithful to SHARING THEIR FOOD.

• They were faithful to the PRAYERS.

• They were faithful to the BREAKING OF THE BREAD.

• They were faithful to the TEACHING OF THE APOSTLES.

With your friends, make a list in your Big Book of Remembering of all the ways that we are faithful to Jesus today.

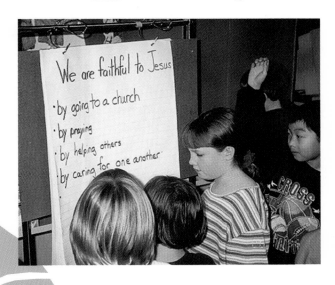

Jesus breathed on the disciples and said to them, "Receive the Holy Spirit."

Words of light

Slowly and secretly the prisoner filled the tiny pieces of paper with the treasures of his heart: "Hear, O Lord and have mercy on me." "We have put our trust in the living God." "Your endurance will win you your lives."

God is our shelter and our strength, always ready to help in times of trouble.

These words from the Bible lit up the darkness for Alfred Delp, brought life and hope to his stark, empty cell. For Alfred Delp was a man of faith, a Jesuit priest who was taken prisoner by the Nazi Gestapo during the Second World War.

For almost five years, Father Delp's country had been at war with most of Europe. He and a group of his friends had been arrested and jailed by the Gestapo – the secret police. They had been blamed for plotting to kill the leader of their country, Adolf Hitler.

In his lonely cell, cut off from his friends and from people, Alfred Delp was lonely and afraid. Most of his personal belongings had been taken from him. Even his Bible had been taken away. His Bible was a precious treasure to Father Delp. When some friends tried to bring him another one, it was not allowed.

The light shines in the darkness, and the darkness has not overcome it.

And yet, amidst all the turmoil, Father Delp was never without the support of God's word. He remembered in his heart and began to write down all the passages of the Bible that came into his mind.

Faced with death, God's word was a source of life and peace for him. Father Delp was like Jesus, who had complete trust in his Father when he, too, was alone and afraid.

"I am the light of the world," he said. "Whoever follows me will have the light of life and will never walk in darkness."

On January 1, 1945, Father Delp wrote these words: "Jesus. The name of our Lord and of my Order shall be the first word I write in the New Year." At the end of the meditation he wrote, "I have pledged myself to Jesus as his loving comrade...." Father Delp was writing the way his heart felt.

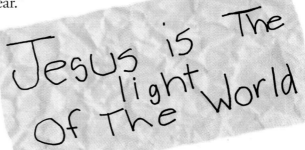

Just one month later, on February 5, 1945, Father Delp was killed. What he wrote in prison, along with the passages of the Bible, live on for us today as words of light, and echo the deep faith of a real martyr, a true witness for Jesus.

When Father Delp wrote his thoughts down on pieces of paper, it was a kind of journalling.

Have you ever kept a journal or diary?

How could it help you?

How do you think it helped Father Delp, his friends and his family?

What promise of Jesus did Father Delp probably remember?

How do you think remembering verses from Scripture helped him?

The word "martyr" means "witness." How is Father Delp a witness to Jesus for us?

Answer this last question in your remembering book and share it with your friends.

From memory to manuscript

I t was discovered early this morning that the sacred writings belonging to the Christian community have all disappeared. Nowhere can any bibles be found! The Christian community is in a state of panic! Alarm is spreading everywhere!

How can we help preserve the story of Jesus? How can we prevent the story from being lost?

Recall your favourite story or quotation from your gospel book and write it down.

Get together with the rest of the class and make a class manuscript out of your work.

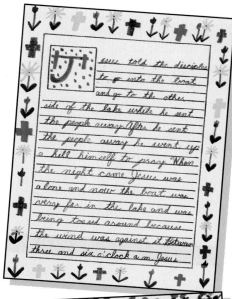

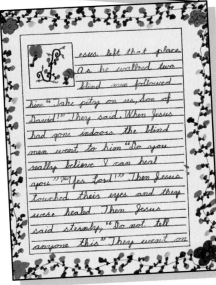

Long ago, when bibles were written out by hand, monks gave their whole lives to copying manuscripts. They worked long and hard to make the Bible pages as beautiful as possible, decorating them with great care and illuminating them with gold leaf.

I have said these things to you while still with you; but the Advocate, the Holy Spirit, whom the Father will send in my name, will teach you everything and remind you of all that I have said to you.

Do you remember this New Testament passage from John 14.25-26?

When did Jesus make this promise to his disciples?

Follow the monks' example and carefully decorate your Bible passage.

Can you imagine how the gospels were put together in the first century?

What would people want to remember and celebrate about Jesus?

How do you think the word of God spread?

How the Gospels came to be

1. Jesus of Nazareth preaches the kingdom of God: 27–30 C.E.

Jesus did not leave us any writings. From what his disciples tell us, his whole life was about doing the work of God. He called it the "kingdom of God." In his words and his actions he showed that this reign of God was coming. He gathered followers and proclaimed to them the gospel – the good news – of God's coming. He died in service of the reign of God.

2. Christians proclaim the risen Christ: from the year 30 on

Although the followers of Jesus ran away when he died, Jesus brought them back together again. He appeared to them after his death. From that point, the disciples proclaimed that God had raised Jesus. They baptized those who believed the good news. They celebrated the death and resurrection of the Lord in the Eucharist.

Those who listened to the word and believed that Jesus was the Christ, the Messiah, were called *Christians*. They formed Christian communities. These communities were called *churches* because they were gatherings or assemblies of God's people.

Little communities of Christians or churches started first in Jerusalem and other parts of the land of Jesus. Then, as the apostles began to travel to Syria, Asia Minor, Greece and Rome, other churches sprang up.

Everywhere they went, the apostles spread the good news about Jesus. They handed on by word of mouth and by signs that in Jesus, God had visited the people. That is why we call the gospel *the teaching of the apostles* or the *apostolic tradition*.

Christians everywhere began to tell the story of Jesus as a story of what God had said and done. Many of the stories were treasured and kept alive in people's memories. The stories were told over and over again whenever the churches gathered.

3. Christians write the gospels of Jesus Christ: 65–100 C.E.

Some of the early followers of Jesus wrote gospels to help these churches live and celebrate the gospel of Jesus Christ. Four gospels came to be read most often in the churches. Today we still proclaim the gospel writings about Jesus by Matthew, Mark, Luke and John. The person of Jesus Christ remains alive and present in our churches.

The evangelists remembered Jesus' promise – "I will send the Spirit of truth to you; the Spirit will guide you into all the truth" (John 16.7, 13). They wrote about the words and actions of Jesus as a Word of God. Soon these writings became part of the Bible, the Book of God's Word.

We take paper for granted – we see large amounts of it every day. But in biblical times, writing materials were much harder to get. That is because they took a long time to make.

A reed called papyrus was cut to show its inner stem. These inside parts were cut into strips and laid out on a hard surface, some lengthwise and some crosswise. Then, the papermaker would crush the stems, hitting them with a mallet until they stuck together, forming a sheet. When the sheet was dry, it was rolled up into a scroll.

Storing a number of scrolls was a problem, because they took up so much room. By about the second century, people discovered that they could flatten sheets of papyrus and hold them together to form a codex, and our present-day book came to be.

The earliest complete manuscript of the New Testament is the Codex Sinaiticus. This manuscript is written in Greek on parchment. It is from the fourth century.

Remember

The gospels are stories to help us keep alive the memory of Jesus.

5 First memories of Jesus: the call to "Come and see"

A special person

Josephine was one of those people you could meet once and remember. She had the most warm, welcoming face I had ever seen. The first time I met her I was nine years old. My family had just moved into the neighbourhood and it was my first day at St. Aloysius School. I dreaded the thought of going into a new place with hundreds of strange eyes staring at me. Even the walls seemed to be watching me as I stumbled into the awesome corridors. The floors were shiny and squeaky clean. That was a welcome change from the last school I had been in. I didn't know where I was going or what I was doing when I opened the first door that had a big sign on it. It read in huge, colourful letters, WHO'S SPECIAL? YOU!

The word YOU was just my height, and as I looked into the letter "O" I saw a reflection of me, since it was shaped out of an oval mirror. I sure looked scared! As I walked in, there was a tiny room with a mop and pail leaning against a large tub and a lot of dusters and cleaning fluids all around. Suddenly, a voice behind me said, "Hi! My name's Josephine and this is my office. Can I help you?"

That was the beginning of my meeting with the custodian of the school. Her eyes were soft and crinkled when she smiled and you could tell by her hands that she had worked long and hard. She made me feel so welcome! Together we set off on a grand tour of the school, ending at my classroom, where she introduced me to my new Grade 4 teacher and soon-to-be friends.

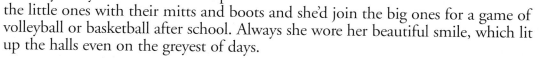

The rest of the day was no longer the frightening experience I thought it would be, and all my other new meetings that day were made much easier because of Josephine. During the rest of the day and in the days to come, I found out just how much she was loved by everyone. She would help the little ones with their mitts and boots and she'd join the big ones for a game of volleyball or basketball after school. Always she wore her beautiful smile, which lit up the halls even on the greyest of days.

That first day I couldn't wait to get home and tell my family about what a great time I'd had in my new school. Josephine was a name I used often after that to tell others about some of the good things that were happening at St. Al's!

Do you know a special person like Josephine?

Where did you meet this person?

How did you feel when you met for the first time?

What did you like about him or her?

Did you come to know him or her better?

What did you tell others about this person?

Did you introduce him or her to your friends?

At Bethany, on the far side of the Jordan River, John the Baptist was baptizing. As he stood there with two of his disciples, Jesus passed by. Staring hard at Jesus, John pointed to him and said, "Look, there is the Lamb of God."

Hearing this, the two disciples – Andrew and John – followed Jesus. Jesus turned around, saw them following and asked, "What do you want?" They answered, "Rabbi" – which means Teacher – "where do you live?"

"Come and see," he replied; so they went and saw where Jesus lived and stayed with him the rest of the day only. (See John 1.35-39.)

Was the "Come and see" invitation for one day?

Early the next morning, Andrew had exciting news for his brother, Simon. "We have found the Messiah!" – which means the Christ – Andrew exclaimed, and he took Simon to Jesus. Jesus looked hard at Simon and said, "You are Simon, son of John; you are to be called Cephas" – meaning Rock.

The next day, after Jesus had decided to leave for Galilee, he met Philip and said to him, "Follow me." Philip came from the same town, Bethsaida, as Andrew and Peter.

Philip found Nathanael and said to him, "We have found the one Moses wrote about in the law, the one about whom the prophets wrote: he is Jesus, son of Joseph, from Nazareth." "From Nazareth?" Nathanael asked. "Can anything good come from that place?" "Come and see," replied Philip. (See John 1.40-46.)

Find Bethsaida, Galilee, Nazareth and the Jordan River on the maps on the inside front and back covers of this book.

What do you think Philip meant when he said, "Come and see"?

Later on, as Jesus was walking throughout Galilee, he met a man named Matthew sitting by the customs house. Jesus said to him, "Follow me." Matthew got up and followed Jesus. (See Matthew 9.9.)

Do you think it was exciting meeting Jesus?
What did Matthew do?
What did Andrew do?
What did Philip do?

Choose your favourite fabric and design a "Come and see" curtain for your drama!

Come and see

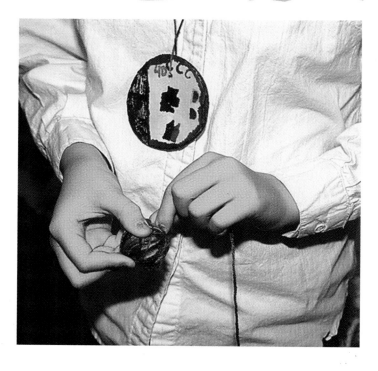

It was just another crisp September morning for Matthew. Just another school day – all except for one thing. Today he and his Grade 4 class were going to reveal the secrets of their pendant codes! Matthew's limp was eager as he made his way to St. Anthony's Elementary in the brisk morning air.

The Grade 4 class had worked hard all week preparing their pendants: making the dough, designing their secret codes, painting them on. They pulled ribbons through tiny holes in the hard dough so they could hang their pendants around their necks. Now the time had come!

The children gathered in a small, cozy circle on the classroom floor. Everything soon grew quiet, except for the glow of the large Christ candle that flickered fast shadows against the classroom wall.

The teacher handed a skein of yarn to the first storyteller, who began to share the secrets of her code. As she told her story to the class, she rolled the yarn into a ball. The storyball grew bigger and bigger as one student, then another, took a turn. All of a sudden Matthew found himself holding the storyball. From the stillness in the room he could tell that the class was anxiously awaiting his story.

Holding the ball of yarn steady in his hand, Matthew stared out at the little circle of people. Somehow he knew that the story he would share today would be the story of a lifetime. Gently he laid the ball in his lap and steadied it with his right paralyzed arm. Matthew reached for the pendant that hung 'round his neck.

"I have chosen an M for my code," he said. "M stands for Matthew, Mary and Mother. This past summer I was able to be with my mom and I was happy. M is special to me."

The number 10 was visible as Matthew slowly turned over his pendant. "Ten years ago, when I was born, I nearly died," Matthew continued. "Ten stands for ten years of life."

His classmates were feeling Matthew's story. "I have something else to say," Matthew blurted, as he let go of the pendant and reached for the storyball. "For a long time I have come to school with my handicap. For a long time I have felt left out and alone."

There was a long, silent pause before Matthew spoke again, and his dark eyes filled with tears.

"Today, as I roll my story, I don't feel left out anymore. For the first time I feel I belong, I belong here. It's the greatest feeling!"

How do you think the class felt after Matthew's story? Do you think they finally understood why Matthew had been silent all those years?

Do you think they told others about what happened?

How is this a "Come and see" story?

Think of ways that the Lord Jesus invites us to follow him today.
Mime your thoughts for your friends.

new words

Rabbi: means "teacher."

messiah: means "Christ" or "the anointed one."

Cephas: means "rock."

Remember

Philip said to his friend Nathanael: "We have found the one Moses and the prophets wrote about. He is Jesus, son of Joseph, from Nazareth." (See John 1.45.)

6 And great crowds followed Jesus

Man in motion

Stroke, stroke, stroke – he covered 16 kilometres per hour. The man of courage and spirit who kept the wheels moving for people with handicaps struck a chord in each of us through his World Tour.

His tour began with a dream of travelling from country to country in his wheelchair. He wanted to give hope to the handicapped by drawing attention to them and their abilities rather than their disabilities. All along his route, he raised money for spinal cord research and wheelchair sports. This meant breaking the barriers of distance, of language and of stamina. In his travels, he met people of peace and people of war, but all dropped their weapons for a brief time to allow him to pass unharmed. Of his project he said, "We've seen the expressions of goodwill, the co-operation, the kindness. Now when I watch television and see news of another war, I know there's hope. Peace on earth is really what everybody wants."

This man is Rick Hansen, an athlete with an iron determination which made him a champion we can admire and have as a hero. What's his secret? He had a dream to get the whole world together to solve a problem. His hope was that his efforts would lessen the pain of others. He gave everything he had so others might live more fully.

Why did he attract the crowds? He had an enthusiasm for life which was contagious. When he stopped to talk to people, they listened because he forgot about his own struggles and focused on the people who helped him make it through each day. His mind and heart opened to those who contributed to his project.

One time during his tour, it was getting close to Christmas. Someone asked him, "If you could have anything you wanted for Christmas, what would it be?" Hansen replied after some thought, "It may be a lot to hope for, but if one of the countries we visited, or even one we didn't visit, announced a new program for the disabled, I would feel very, very good about it." He could have wished for anything for himself: to get better, to feel less tired, to be in a warmer country; instead, his wish was for others. He wanted to fulfill a dream that would ensure that those with disabilities would be treated more kindly and have their talents recognized.

The end of the day for Rick always brought pain and exhaustion. However, he had a way of talking only about his dream. "I have a dream that some day, I will see people getting up out of their wheelchairs and walking."

Would you go to see Rick Hansen if he came to your town? Why?

Would you want him to notice you?

What would you do to attract his attention?

What would you say to him if you had a chance to talk to him?

What do you think was the message of his journey?

Do you know people like Rick who draw crowds because of their strong spirit?

Create your very own story cube with stories and drawings of the special people you know.

Great crowds gather around Jesus

Look these passages up in your Bible and finish reading about the events.

"The whole city was gathered together about the door" (Mark 1.33)

"So many people collected that there was no room left, even in front of the door" (Mark 2.2)

"They were bringing children to him" (Mark 10.13ff)

"He went up on the mountain and called to him those whom he desired; and they came to him" (Mark 3.13)

"Again he began to teach by the sea. And a very large crowd gathered about him, so that he got into a boat and sat in it on the sea" (Mark 4.1)

For more crowd stories, read these:

- Mark 1.35-38
- Mark 2.13
- Mark 3.31
- Mark 1.40-45
- Mark 3.7-10
- Mark 6.30-44

What is it about Jesus that makes people want to meet him?

Remember

"Who do you say that I am?" "You are the Messiah." (Mark 8.29)

46

Unit 3
Jesus tells us about the reign of God

Theme 7   Jesus is a storyteller
Theme 8   Jesus the parabler
Theme 9   Parables are kingdom stories

7 Jesus is a storyteller

Totem poles

Long ago, the native peoples of Canada's northwest coast spent long hours constructing totem poles to tell their stories. Their lives and their beliefs are documented on these poles!

Totem poles were made from tall cedar trees. Skilled artists carved the long logs and painted them, using paints made from fish oil, berry root, charcoal and other natural ingredients.

Totems belonged to the families who put them up. The carved figures on a family totem pole represented the names, rights and possessions of the family. The figures helped the family remember its stories and traditions. Totem pole figures were carved to look like humans, birds and animals. The animals often displayed human faces and hands, sitting or standing up straight like human beings.

It was a time of great celebration when a totem pole was ready to be raised and set upright in the village. People gathered to feast and to dance. They gathered especially to hear the family storyteller tell stories about the figures on the pole.

Today, families are holding onto their tradition and carving new poles on Canada's Pacific coast. They are coming together to feast, dance and share stories at the raising of the totem poles.

**Get together with your
friends and find out all you
can about totem poles.**

What figures would you carve on a totem pole?
What experiences and events would you document?
What stories would you want to remember?

**Sketch and paint a totem of your own.
Share the painting with your friends first.
Then bring it home to share and display in a special place.**

Jesus and parables

Jesus was a fantastic storyteller. He used parables to tell stories about God, about God's reign and about people. Jesus used parables like the native peoples you read about used totems to tell stories about life. Parables are to Jesus what totems are for the west coast people.

Parables are like windows through which we see God at the heart of life; in yeast and mustard seeds, in pearls and wheat. Parables help us see with new eyes God's dream of a world filled with peace, justice and love.

"Hear the Word, accept it and bear fruit."

The kingdom of heaven is like the spoonful of yeast that you spill into the bread mix. But what happens to the bread mix? (See Matthew 13.33.)

The kingdom of heaven is like treasure hidden in a field. But what happens when someone finds the treasure? (See Matthew 13.44-46.)

The kingdom of heaven is like a mustard seed. But what happens to a mustard seed when we plant it in the earth? (See Matthew 13.31-32.)

Do you remember these parables? Look them up in your Bible.

The sower

Every picture tells a story. Do you know the story that this picture tells? It is found in your Bible, in the New Testament.

Using the picture as a guide, write the story and tell it at home.

new word

parables: stories of ordinary, everyday events that Jesus used to tell us about God and about God's reign.

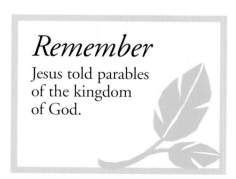

Remember

Jesus told parables of the kingdom of God.

8 Jesus the parabler

Guess what's going on!

Open your remembering book and write down your guess.

Now, go to the New Testament in your Bible and read these parables:
- Luke 15.8-9
- Luke 18.10-13
- Mark 4.26-29

Compare what you wrote with what you read.

A treasure hunt!

Do you have something that is precious to you? a letter? a photo? a book?
Read about the treasures on this page. They come from all across Canada.

Labrador

This letter is my treasure. It was written to me by my grandmother. She was my best friend.

Prince Edward Island

This photo is my treasure. Cathy is with me at the seashore. She's my best friend. It's our first vacation together.

Ontario

Our piano is a treasure for me. I have played it for a long time and it has been in our family for many years.

Saskatchewan

These seeds are my treasure. They come from our first garden. I helped my family plant it last spring.

Seabottom treasures

If you have ever seen or held a pearl, no doubt you understand why people think they are such treasures. Pearls are smooth and cool and milky white but with faint touches of colour, too. People the world over agree: pearls are very beautiful.

Pearls form inside oysters, which live at the bottom of the sea. If you could open an oyster shell, you would see that it is lined with a pearly coating called mother-of-pearl.

Sometimes, a grain of sand gets inside the living oyster's shell. This causes the little creature some discomfort, so it begins to cover the sand with a layer of pearly

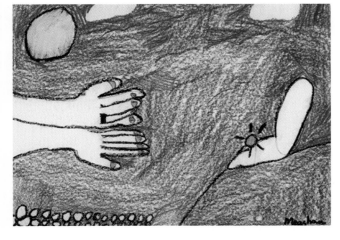

material called "nacre." It also rolls the sand around and around, trying to get it right out of the shell.

Over a long time, the nacre-covered sand becomes very round and hard – a pearl, in fact. The longer it is in the oyster's shell, the larger it grows and the rounder it becomes. Perhaps someday a very lucky person finds the oyster and opens it up to find a valuable treasure. What a surprise!

In your opinion, what makes pearls so precious?

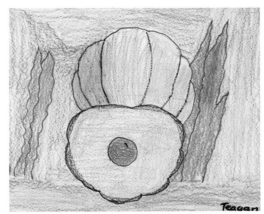

A Jesus parable

"Again, the kingdom of heaven is like a merchant in search of fine pearls; who, on finding one pearl of great value, went and sold all that he had and bought it."

(Matthew 13.45-46)

In this parable, the merchant gives up everything he owns when he finds the pearl of great price.

Imagine that you are in the crowd listening to Jesus.

What might you say to your friend next to you?

Would you ask whether she or he would sell all for the kingdom of God?

What do you think of Jesus as a parabler?

What do you think of the disciples who left everything to follow Jesus?

For them Jesus was such a pearl. To what would you compare Jesus?

Elizabeth was excited, being in the great cathedral for the first time. The stained glass windows held her interest. Deep reds and blues and greens seemed warm and friendly with the sun streaming through to make them bright.

Her mother, seeing Elizabeth's excited look, explained the story behind each pane of glass. She told Elizabeth that, in the days when people could not read books, they could understand the story of a saint's life by looking at the beautiful glass windows in the church.

The next day at school, Elizabeth's teacher wanted to know, "Does anyone know who a saint is?"

Elizabeth was ready with her answer. "A saint is someone the light shines through!"

Do you know people today whose lives show us that they have found the pearl of great price?

Stained glass windows tell the story of our faith. They tell stories about people who have found a great treasure – God's love for them. Over 700 years ago, a man named Richard, who lived in Chichester, England, discovered this treasure. He wrote this prayer and said it every day to remind himself of God's love:

> Day by day,
> Dear Lord, of thee
> Three things I pray:
> To see thee more clearly,
> Love thee more dearly,
> Follow thee more nearly,
> Day by day.

The people who knew Richard saw how good and kind he was to everyone. The light of God's Spirit shone through him in love. This is why, not very long after he died, the Church proclaimed him a saint. He is now known as Saint Richard of Chichester.

Design your own stained glass window of a favourite saint or of the patron of your parish or school. Display it in your parish church.

Read this story about Mother Teresa of Calcutta, India, and see the light of God's love shine through.

Once in the streets of Calcutta I picked up a little girl. She was about six years old and I could tell from her face that she was hungry and hadn't eaten for days. I gave her a crust of bread and she started to eat it, slowly, one crumb at a time. I said to her, "Eat the bread, go on, eat it." And the child replied, "I am afraid, because when the bread is finished I shall be hungry all over again."

In our schools in Calcutta we give free bread and milk to all the children. I noticed one day that a little girl took her bread and hid it. I asked her why she was not eating the bread and she told me: "My mother is very sick at home. We have no food in the house at all and I want to take this bread for her to eat."

"That is real love, real sharing," said Mother Teresa. "Children could learn from that."

Once a little boy from a wealthy family in Calcutta was having a birthday. His parents always gave him a lot of presents and a big party. One year he asked them to give all the money they would spend on him to Mother Teresa. And on the morning of his birthday they brought him down in the car. He handed me an envelope with the money in it.

That child taught his parents so much. He taught them that sharing is love in action. Many children in Calcutta now do not invite their own friends to a birthday party. They come instead to our Children's Home and have the party there with our children as guests.

Mother Teresa smiled. "Tell children how important it is to share," she said. "Tell them that sharing is the most important thing in the world!"

(Mary Craig © Hamish Hamilton Ltd.)

 How do you know that Mother Teresa has found the pearl of great price?

Design a banner with her message. Together with your friends, decide on a special place to hang it so that many people will read it.

Remember

"…the kingdom of heaven is like a merchant in search of fine pearls…" (Matthew 13.45-46)

9 Parables are kingdom stories

Working as a shepherd

"Sheep always know," says D'Alfonso, "that before they lie down for the night, their shepherd has figured out their grazing for tomorrow." Bedded down beside a pool of sparkling water under a clear, starry sky, the sheep feel safe, knowing that their shepherd is with them.

Many of us have seen pictures of sheep with their shepherd, but few of us have actually met a shepherd guiding his flock. In Palestine, where Jesus lived, a shepherd would have been with his sheep from the time he was a young boy. So he was close to them, just as you might be close to one of your pets.

Shepherds name their sheep and know each one by name. The sheep, in turn, know their shepherd, the sound of his voice, the sound of his flute. Shepherds would do anything to protect their sheep, even die if they had to – and sometimes that's just what happened in Palestine. A short time ago, a young shepherd was on his way from Tiberias to Tabor with his sheep when the flock was attacked. Trying to defend his sheep, the shepherd died and was left on the roadside with his dead herd.

At every sheepfold you will find a big earthen bowl of olive oil and a large stone jar of water. As the sheep come in for the night, they are led to a gate. The shepherd stretches his rod across the top of the gateway just higher than the back of the sheep. As each sheep passes in single file, he examines it for injuries. If he finds one, he drops his rod across the sheep's back and the sheep steps out of line. The shepherd then carefully cleans the wound of his injured sheep. Dipping his hand into the olive oil, he anoints the injury. Following this, he brings a cup of cool water – never half full but always overflowing – to the sheep. Sinking its nose into the water up to its eyes, the fevered sheep drinks.

When all the sheep are at rest, the shepherd lays his staff on the ground, wraps himself in his woolen robe and lies across the gateway facing his sheep. With his staff within reach, the shepherd closes his eyes for the night.

J esus wanted to tell us how much God loves us. In a parable he said that God loves us the way a good shepherd loves his sheep. Here are some of the words from this parable of the good shepherd:

Truly, truly, I say to you,
I am the door of the sheep...
if anyone enters by me,
*   he will be saved*
and will go in and out and
*   find pasture.*

I am the good shepherd;
I know my own and my own know me,
as the Father knows me and
I know the Father;
and I lay down my life for the sheep."

(John 10.7-15)

Look up John 10.1-15 in your Bible and read the parable. Why do you think Jesus chose this parable to describe his message?

Make a list in your Big Book of Remembering of all the reasons you think Jesus might have had for using this parable.

The Lord is my shepherd,
*   I shall not want;*
he makes me lie down in
*   green pastures.*
He leads me beside still waters;
he restores my soul.
He leads me in paths
*   of righteousness*
for his name's sake.

Even though I walk through the
*   valley of the shadow of death,*
I fear no evil;
for you are with me;
your rod and your staff,
they comfort me.

You prepare a table before me
in the presence of my enemies;
you anoint my head with oil,
my cup overflows.
Surely goodness and mercy shall follow me
all the days of my life;
and I shall dwell in the house
*   of the Lord for ever.*

(See Psalm 23.)

Sheep graze from around sunrise until late morning. Then they lie down for three or four hours. The shepherd knows that during the resting period, the sheep are putting on fat. The wise shepherd saves the best grazing grounds for the resting time and the sheep flourish in the shady green pastures.

Sheep do not like to drink gurgling water from fast-flowing streams. High in the hills of Israel, a shepherd often fashions with his hand a little pool of water for his sheep – enough perhaps to hold a bucketful.

During the day, a sheep often leaves its grazing and goes to the shepherd. The shepherd rubs the sheep's nose, scratches its ear. After a few minutes the sheep returns to its grazing.

South of the Jericho Road leading from Jerusalem to the Dead Sea, there is a narrow, dangerous valley through a mountain range. The sheep must pass through this for seasonal feeding.

The valley is over seven kilometres long. Its sidewalls are over 500 metres high in places, and it is only three or four metres wide at the bottom. Travelling through the valley is dangerous because its floor is cut with deep gullies. The sheep must jump across. The shepherd coaxes the sheep to take the leap; if they slip, he uses his staff to catch them. The old-style crook is encircled around a large sheep's neck or a small sheep's chest, and the sheep is lifted to safety!

On the grazing grounds there are poisonous plants. Each spring the shepherd must be constantly alert. Going ahead of the flock, he carefully weeds out the poisonous roots.

In the evening, the injured sheep are cared for with olive oil and cool, fresh water.

Safe inside the fold, the shepherd and the sheep lie down for the night.

The Lord is your shepherd.

Remember

"I am the good shepherd. The good shepherd lays down his life for the sheep." (John 10.11)

WANTED:
strong and healthy people
to train as shepherds.

REQUIREMENTS:
must like animals and the
outdoors; enjoy being on
the trail for long periods
of time; and be willing to
lay down their lives for
their sheep.

Apply in writing or
come in person to:

Shepherds Inc.
R.R. # 1
Antigonish, Nova Scotia

Unit 4
A light shines in the darkness

10 A light shines in the darkness

A light in the darkness

"Bet you can't hit that tree with a snowball!" John teases Tommy.

"Bet I can!" Tommy teases back as he lets go of his toboggan and positions himself to fire at the white smudgy oak. Whack! The snowball splatters. And the two friends continue to tease each other as they trudge along in the dry, crisp snow.

"I like winter," John says. "I like snow and snowballs and tobogganing."

"I love tobogganing! It's my favourite!" Tommy is excited. "Hey, let's really go tobogganing!" he exclaims. "I'll beat you to the hill!"

"You mean the big hill?" John asks his friend with half a stare.

"Yes, the big one – Ice Mountain! Let's make it the best afternoon ever. We can do it. I know we can." Tommy's voice bubbles with excitement. "Ice Mountain is too far," John thinks to himself. "It's mid-afternoon and the woods across the valley are thick." For a moment he is silent. Then he catches the glow in Tommy's eyes and he begins to feel the adventure of the big hill. "Okay, we'll do it!" And off they go towards Ice Mountain Peak with their toboggans trailing behind them.

On the far side of the valley, the trail is hard to see, but the sun is still strong.

Soon Ice Mountain is before them! And the fun begins. Time passes quickly as they slide up and down and down and up the steep icy slopes. Their laughter bounces over the hills and breaks the silence of the crisp winter air.

Suddenly, Tommy yells to his friend, "Hey, John, it's getting dark! Why is it getting dark so soon?" John realizes that it's way past the time to go. They were having so much fun that they hadn't even noticed the time. They hadn't noticed the snowflakes that were now falling fast.

"Remember at Hallowe'en, Tommy, how long we had to wait before it got dark? There's more night and less light every day now. Isn't that strange?"

"Sort of scary," Tommy replies. "Suppose every day it got darker and darker and one day the sun never came back."

"But it couldn't. We learned about that in science, remember?"

As the boys walk on, they feel a soft wind on their back. And there are no stars in the sky. They enter the thick woods and pick their way through the tall trees. "The path must be over here," says John, hoping to find an opening in the dense brush.

"I think we're lost," Tommy wails. "And I'm scared."

The woods are darker now and the trees cast giant shadows. Without any light and with the snow falling, every trace of a trail is gone. "There's a storm blowing up," John says. "Do you feel the wind?" Their hearts beat faster now as they begin to hear sounds they have never heard before.

All at once, a huge lightning bolt strikes across their path. Icy pebbles begin to hit hard. Thunder crashes through the forest. The two boys crouch under some low branches, shuddering. All they can do now is wait in the darkness.

When the wind seems to let up, John is the first to speak. "We've got to get out of here and move on," he says. Tommy trembles at the thought. They begin to pick their way through the shadowy darkness once more.

Slowly, slowly a soft, dim glow sets in between the shadows of the trees. "It must be the moon," John says. All at once Tommy yells, "Look, John, look!" There, above a little clearing in the woods, is the most beautiful star-dotted sky the boys have ever seen. The moon streams down to light their way. "We can do it now, Tommy. I know the way." John's voice is strong again. Quick as fireflies, the boys head for home.

At home that night Tommy wanted to talk about light. He asked his mom the same question he had asked John: "What if the sun left us forever?"

"It won't do that," his mom assured him. "The sun stands still, Tommy, and the earth revolves around it year after year. In winter the days get shorter and the nights get longer. But the time of light always comes back again. It's the earth moving, Tommy. The sun is not running away."

His mom continued. "Long ago, the short, dark days used to frighten people. They didn't know that the time of sunlight would return. They were afraid of every winter, just like you were tonight."

"I bet they were glad when spring came back again. That's how I felt when I came in the door tonight – like it was spring."

"Light and warmth do that for you." His mother was thoughtful for a minute. "Light is like a promise fulfilled, when you think about it. A candle is just a promise, until it is lit. Then the light shines out, the darkness disappears, and everyone feels good."

"That's how we felt tonight when the moon lit the way for us," Tommy said. "We felt safe again!"

"People have lots of ways of making themselves feel good at the time of year when it's bleak and dark. People all over the world give thanks for light coming out of the darkness. Chinese New Year has lanterns and dragons and firecrackers. In India, there's the Feast of Divali, when little lamps are hung in the windows and even floated down rivers. And Jewish people have Hanukkah, the Festival of Lights. Then there's Christmas – you know all about that, I suppose?"

Tommy smiled, thinking about Christmas, which was just a few more weeks away. "There will be presents and songs and food and..."

"And lots of light, warmth and love," his mother finished for him. "Now go to sleep! This light's going out and that's it!"

"But not forever. Goodnight, Mom."

Paint your favourite scene from the story.
Choose a word or sentence to go with it and create a shadow box.

Why was Tommy afraid?

What do you think the boys were wishing for?

What helped them find their way home?

How is a candle like a promise?

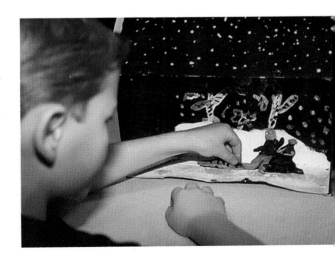

66

Whedn Father Herbert Dunlop of Vancouver, British Columbia, heard that you would be reflecting on light and darkness in this theme, he sat down and wrote you a message:

"In your story you have talked of light and darkness; the darkness that comes upon the world when the sun goes down; darkness that makes us afraid to be alone.

"But there is another kind of darkness. It has nothing to do with the sun going down in the evening...."

What does Father Dunlop mean?
Share your thoughts with your friends.

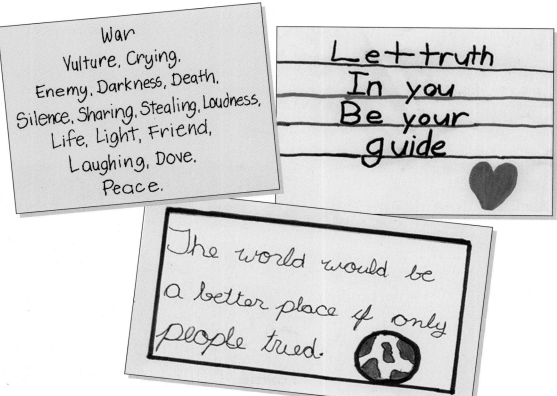

War
Vulture, Crying,
Enemy, Darkness, Death,
Silence, Sharing, Stealing, Loudness,
Life, Light, Friend,
Laughing, Dove,
Peace.

Let truth
In you
Be your
guide

The world would be a better place if only people tried.

T ime is running out! Christmas is just around the corner! Christians call this special waiting time Advent. It is getting-ready time, a time of hope. It is a time of waiting in hope for light!

The Advent wreath is round, with no beginning and no end, just like God's love.

The wreath is made of evergreen branches, which stay green even in winter and remind us of the gift of life.

The wreath has four candles – one for each week of Advent. As we light one more candle each week, we can see how we are getting closer to celebrating Jesus' coming.

Gathering

Lighting of the candle

Blessing of the Advent wreath

Dear God,
We praise you, gracious God,
as we begin this Advent season.
Bless us as we light this wreath.
May its light shine in our lives.
We ask this through Jesus Christ our Lord.
Amen.

Word of God

Alleluia, Alleluia, Alleluia, Alleluia,
Come prepare a way for the Lord
All shall see the salvation of our God

Ritual action

Ritual Action

My hope for a better world!

Closing prayer

Dear God,
during this time of Advent
help us to get ready
to celebrate the coming of Jesus,
*   your Word,*
at the first Christmas long ago
and in our lives today. Amen.

How are you and your friends making the light and hope of Advent come alive?

John the Baptist is a sign of hope

For hundreds of years before the coming of Jesus, people were longing for the light, longing for signs of hope in the darkness of their lives.

"And then the word of God came to John, son of Zechariah and Elizabeth," Luke's Gospel tells us. John was living the life of a hermit in the wilderness of Judaea when this happened.

In the fifteenth year of the reign of Tiberias Caesar (about 27 C.E.), John knew in his heart that he was to be God's message of hope.

On the banks of the Jordan River, his message sounded forth:

"Prepare the way of the Lord, make his paths straight."

"Prepare the way of the Lord, make his paths straight."

Decorate John's message and hang it in a special place in your home.

new word

Advent: means "coming."

Remember

"Prepare the way of the Lord, make his paths straight." (Luke 3.4)

11 John the Baptist bears witness to the light

"Repent, for the kingdom of heaven is close at hand."

The crowds who followed John the Baptist saw that he was very serious about what he had to say. His message was urgent because he was speaking for God.

John the Baptist was a great prophet who spoke out strongly in God's name. "Someone who is mightier than I is coming," said John, "the thong of whose sandals I am not worthy to untie" (Luke 3.16).

John made people look at the darkness and sin in their lives. Longing in their hearts for the light that John promised, they asked him, "What must we do?" "Repent, for the kingdom of heaven is close at hand," John said.

During Advent we also ask, "What must we do? How can we get ready to welcome the promised one, the true light?"

Meet Jenny and Joey

Joey: What on earth happened to *you*?

Jenny: What do you mean?

Joey: Your hair. . . !

Jenny: I'll have you know I paid a lot of money for this haircut!

Joey: I didn't mean to upset you, but your hair looked great just the way it was.

Jenny: Thanks, but I had to change it.

Joey: What makes you say that?

Jenny: Don't you know what time of the year this is?

Joey: Of course I do. It's December!

Jenny: Besides that – What time of the church year is it?

Joey: It's Advent – one of my favourite times because of all the special things we do to get ready for Christmas.

Jenny: And Advent is a time for us to change. Don't you remember Father Don's homily last Sunday about John the Baptist? He said that John told people to prepare the way of the Lord by changing.

Joey: So *that's* it! But John the Baptist didn't mean changing on the outside – things like your hairstyle or your clothes. He meant changing on the inside in the way that you love God and other people.

Jenny: But how are people going to know that I've changed on the inside?

Joey: They'll know by the good things that you do.

**Write in your remembering book one way you can "change on the inside."
Make up an Advent puppet show and share it with your family and friends.**

new words

prophet: a person who speaks for God.

repent: to "change our hearts" or "turn around."

Remember

John came for testimony, to bear witness to the light. (See John 1.7.)

12 We celebrate the light shining in the darkness

In a world made dark by sin,
O God of compassion,
You made John the Baptist
    announce
the coming of Christ, the Light
    of the world.
Straighten the winding ways
    of our hearts
smooth the paths made rough
    by sin.
Give us a spirit of repentance
    that we may see his light
in our hearts and actions.

"There shall come forth a shoot from the stump of Jesse and a branch shall grow out of its roots and the Spirit of the Lord shall rest upon him..."
(Isaiah 11.1-2)

God is with us

In the Byzantine–Ukrainian Church, the Christmas Eve service is celebrated with great rejoicing. When the priest sings out the proclamation, "God is with us," a feeling of exultation fills the church and people sing over and over again, "God is with us… rejoice… God is with us!"

God is truly with us. God is with us, a child is born to us: a Light has shone on us, a Light for all nations. God is with us in Jesus, whose name is Emmanuel.

Leader: *God is with us. Give ear all you nations and be humbled, for God is with us. Upon us who dwell in the land of the shadow of death a great light has shone.*

Response: *God is with us. Give ear all you nations, and be humbled, for God is with us.*

Leader: *For a child is born to us, a Son is given to us.*

Response: *God is with us. Give ear all you nations, and be humbled, for God is with us.*

Leader: *God's power is upon his shoulder and his peace shall have no end.*

Response: *God is with us. Give ear all you nations, and be humbled, for God is with us.*

Leader: *And he shall be called the messenger of the great wisdom of God.*

Response: *God is with us. Give ear all you nations, and be humbled, for God is with us.*

Leader: *Wonderful, Counselor, the Mighty God, the Master, the Prince of Peace, the Father of the age to come.*

Response: *God is with us. Give ear all you nations, and be humbled, for God is with us.*

(Adapted from the great compline of the Feast of the Nativity of Christ)

We are children,
children of the light,
We are shining,
in the darkness of the night,
Hope for this world,
Joy through all the land,
Touch the heart of ev'ryone,
Take ev'rybody's hand.

Pray this prayer when you light the fourth Advent candle:

The brightness of our wreath,
God of mystery,
reflects the light of Jesus Christ.
May the birth of Jesus
cast away the darkness of sin
and bathe us in new light.
We ask this through
       Jesus Christ our Lord.
Amen.

Remember

Jesus is the Light
of the world.

Unit 5
Jesus, "born of a woman"

13 Jesus, born of a woman

Look at the scenes on this page.

What do they remind you of?

How do these actions help light up Christmas?

Who helped
light up your
Christmas?

**Write a letter to thank that
person for helping to light up
your Christmas.**

T his is Israel – the homeland of Jesus. How long would it take to travel to Israel from where you are? by jet? by boat?

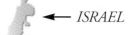 *ISRAEL*

**The two maps to the left compare the size of Israel to the size of Canada.
Use a roadmap to measure from your town to another town about 240 kilometres away. That's about the length of Israel!**

CANADA

Israel is special to many people. For Jewish people, it is a homeland. For Christians, it is special, too. Each year, thousands of people go to Israel to visit the places where Jesus lived and walked. Some of those journeys are called pilgrimages.

 Do you know anyone who has made a pilgrimage to Israel? What did they like best about their trip?

Let's go on a pilgrimage!

Beautiful Galilee was Jesus' home

Jesus was born in Bethlehem, but he spent almost all his life in the region of Galilee in the north. Unlike the south, Galilee at that time was the "garden" of Palestine. On his travels, Jesus would have seen fields of golden wheat, green olive groves, grape vineyards and orchards of fig and other fruit trees. Palestine's wine, wheat and olive oil were exported all over the Roman Empire. Most Galileans were poor farmers who worked a small plot of land for a small share of the harvest. Jesus knew these people well and loved them.

Here is the Sea of Galilee

This lake was probably called the "Sea" of Galilee (or Tiberias) because it was the only large body of water in the north. It is about 24 kilometres long and 11 kilometres wide. The centre of the fishing industry, the lake was always crowded with fishing boats, especially at night. Jesus loved the Sea of Galilee.

Jerusalem is now in view

Jerusalem was the largest city in Palestine. It was built in the high hills overlooking the countryside below. Jerusalem had a great history, for the leaders of the Jewish people had lived here and defended it against invaders. It was in this city that one of their kings, named Solomon, had built the most beautiful temple in which to worship God.

Archaeologists are men and women who try to find out about people who lived long ago by studying what these people left behind – like buildings, tools and dishes.

Archaeologists have been able to tell us much about the land of Jesus through their excavations, or digs. With their help and the writings of ancient times, read some interesting information on the next pages about life in Galilee.

Workers in Jesus' time

Fishermen, potters, merchants and carpenters did very important work in Jesus' time. Fish was one of the main sources of food, so fishermen were special. Good fishermen worked long, hard hours. Sometimes they didn't catch anything, but they kept trying. In the morning, they sorted the fish into baskets. Some fish would go to the market. Some were dried and salted for export. Can you remember the names of Jesus' disciples who were fishermen?

Another important trade in Nazareth was pottery making. Potters made things that people needed in their daily lives. We can imagine that Jesus watched the village potter shaping lumps of clay on his potter's wheel into bowls, water jugs and small oil lamps. The potter would then put them to dry in the sun or fire them in kilns. By studying pottery they find on their digs, archaeologists learn about life in ancient Palestine.

Carpenters also made things for people to use, such as furniture and tools. Joseph was a carpenter, so Jesus would have known this trade well. With simple tools he would have helped Joseph make such things as tables, benches, stools, door frames, yokes for animals and ploughs. Carpenters also made toys for children, such as tops for spinning.

The marketplace in a village like Nazareth was rich in sights and smells and sounds – especially on Friday morning before the Sabbath. People came from all over to set up their stalls and sell their wares. What do you think Jesus would have seen, smelled and heard there?

Take a look at this present-day photo. The market is still quite a busy place.

In Jesus' day, the women came and went to the village well for water. There is still a well in Nazareth today, called "Mary's Well."

At home and at school

At home, Jesus spoke a language called Aramaic. As a small boy he would have learned much from his mother and from the Jewish rituals held in the home.

When Jesus was six years old, he would have already started going to school with other boys. School was held in the synagogue, often called the "House of the Book." There the boys would sit on a mat around their rabbi or teacher. They learned to read the Torah from a hand-written Torah scroll. They learned to read and recite much of it in a kind of sing-song Hebrew chant. At the end of the day they would listen to the rabbi tell them wonderful stories about their people.

Playing games

Children in Jesus' day made up their own games. For example, they would dig a hole in the ground and see how many stones they could throw into the hole from a certain distance. They would also pretend they were adults, playing wedding, house and funeral. (See Matthew 11.16-17.)

In Jesus' day, the houses had very simple furnishings – the one room was both a living room and kitchen. Mats for sleeping were rolled up during the day. Every home had a pottery lamp that burned olive oil, and even in the poorest home this was kept burning all night.

The poorer people had one-room houses made of handmade, sun-dried bricks. The floors were mostly earthen, packed hard and worn smooth. The rooftop was flat, with a low wall around it. Most people used a ladder or outside stairway to climb onto the roof. Here the family spread grain and fruits to dry in the hot sun. When the weather was good, people did their chores on the roof. Every morning, Mary probably ground grain for bread there on the rooftop. This was also a cool place to sleep.

Here is a picture of Nazareth today.

Take a look at the photo to see some of the foods you would eat while on a pilgrimage in Israel. If you had a meal with a Jewish family, you might hear this blessing:

Blessed are you, Lord,
God of all creation,
for you feed the whole world
with your goodness, with grace,
with loving kindness and
tender mercy. You give food
to all creatures, and your
loving kindness endures forever.
Blessed are you, O Lord!

This Grade 4 class has prepared a meal of pita bread, bagels, cream cheese, matzahs, honey, cheese, hummos, fruit, nuts, vegetables, olive oil, milk, water and grape juice.

A Palestinian village!

Remember

With the child and his mother, Joseph went to the province of Galilee and made his home in a village called Nazareth. (See Matthew 2.21-23.)

new word

pilgrimage: a special journey to holy places.

14 Jesus is presented in the Temple

The Presentation Song

When Simeon first saw
  Mary's child
His heart was filled with
  radiance bright;
He held him in his arms and sang
In praise of Jesus, child of light.
"Now I can die a happy man
My eyes have seen the
  wondrous sight
Of Jesus who will save
  the world,
The long awaited light of light."
Still Jesus shines upon our way,
And shows us how to live aright.
We hold our candles high
  and sing
In praise of Jesus, Lord of light.

From *Live, Learn and Worship*
(CIO Publishing),
© 1979 The Wadderton Group.
Reproduced by permission.

The National Gallery of Canada

Joseph and Mary remember

"I remember," Mary said eagerly. "How could I forget! It was such a special day. We took Jesus to Jerusalem to present him to the Lord."

"I remember Simeon." Joseph's voice was clear. "It was just a wonderful scene. Simeon took Jesus in his arms and blessed God; and he said: 'My eyes have seen the salvation which you have prepared for all the nations to see.'"

JH (News reporter): Who did you meet when you entered the Temple?

Mary: Simeon and Anna.

JH: Tell us what you remember about Simeon.

Mary: He was a very holy man who prayed special prayers for Jesus.

It seems Mary and Joseph were very impressed with Anna and Simeon. They kept saying Simeon's words all through the interview:

"Thank you, God, for keeping your promise. Now I am happy to die, for I have seen Jesus, the light of the world!"

Blessed be the Holy Spirit who gathers us today
Blessed be Jesus the light of the world
Blessed be God, Father, Son and Holy Spirit.
We ask you to bless the candles we have made
and bless our class
who joyfully carry them
in praise of your name.

Star
Sparkly, Shiny
Glowing, dazzling, loving.
Our light
Jesus.

By: Jason.

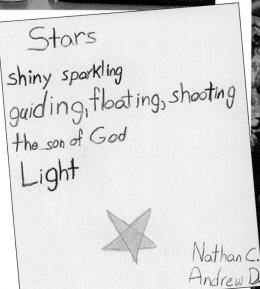

Stars
shiny sparkling
guiding, floating, shooting
the son of God
Light

Nathan C.
Andrew D.

Shine upon us today
O God, the source of all light.
Brightened by the glow of these candles
may we recognize your Son, Jesus, in the word;
and, like Anna and Simeon,
may we welcome him into our lives
and joyfully proclaim him to the world.

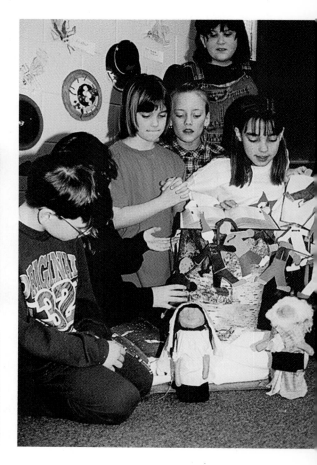

Remember

Simeon and Anna welcomed
Jesus, the light of the world.

15 When Jesus was 12 years old

Imagine that you were in the Temple with Jesus. In your remembering book, write an account of what happened.

Get together with your friends and compare your accounts.

When we enter special, holy places, we often feel reverent. Read this story in the Bible about Moses' experience in a holy place:

One day, Moses was taking care of some sheep on the mountainside. Suddenly, he noticed fire coming from the middle of a bush. The bush was on fire, but it did not burn up! Moses said to himself, "I must go and look at this strange sight and see why the bush is not burned." As he came closer, he heard God call his name, "Moses! Moses!" He answered, "Here I am." "Come no nearer," the Lord said. "Take off your shoes, for the place on which you stand is holy ground. I am the God of your father, the God of Abraham, the God of Jacob."
(See Exodus 3.1-6.)

Here are some special places. Why do you think they are sacred?

Do you have a sacred place?

How do you feel when you go there?

Jewish people have sacred places. The synagogue and the home are the two main places of prayer and worship.

For centuries, the Temple in Jerusalem was the most important "House of Prayer." Twice the enemies of the Jewish people came and destroyed it.

When Jesus grew up, the second temple was still being built. Today, all that is left of this second temple in Jerusalem is one wall, called the Western Wall. For Jewish people it is the holiest place on earth. Many go there to pray.

The Jewish people do not have their temple. "But," they say, "we will always be able to keep our faith as long as we have our Torah."

S haring a Sabbath (Shabbat) or Passover meal together is a sacred time for Jews. It is a time when special events are remembered and celebrated. That is why the family table is a holy place.

Can you identify the foods on the table? Find out why these foods are eaten at the Passover Seder.

When Jesus first got up in the morning, he would have said, *"Baruch Adonai"* (ba'rook a'-do-ni), which means "Blessed be the Lord." He would have said other blessings when he washed and dressed and had his breakfast. But the most important morning prayer he would have learned is called the Shema (shay-ma). "Shema" is the first word of the prayer. It means "Listen!"

"Hear, O Israel, The Lord our God is the one God. You shall love our God with all your heart, with all your soul, and with all your strength." (Deuteronomy 6.4-5)

This prayer is repeated in the evening. In Jesus' day, parents taught these words to their children. They wrote them on parchment, put them in tiny boxes called phylacteries (phil-ac-ter-eez) and wore them on their left arm and forehead. The words of the Shema are also kept in the *mezuzah*.

A mezuzah, which means "doorpost," is on the doorways of most Jewish homes. This small case contains a tiny, rolled-up piece of parchment with a verse from the Torah on it. People touch the mezuzah reverently as they go in and out and say this prayer: "The Lord God will guard my going and my coming, now and forevermore" (Psalm 121).

After Jesus rolled up his sleeping mat, he would have watched Joseph tie his phylacteries on his left arm and forehead. Then Joseph would have put on his prayer shawl, or *tallith* and recited the morning prayers to God.

Jewish people today use these shawls during prayer. Women and girls do not have to pray at special times or wear a prayer shawl or skull cap (*yarmulke*) when they pray. But many want to do this. They say that putting on a tallith is like entering the "tent of God" to pray. It is like going into a holy place where one feels protected. It is like resting in the palm of God's hand.

A holy day

The third commandment of the Lord is this: "Remember to keep holy the Sabbath day." Many Jewish people today observe this law quite strictly. It is a day of rest and prayer. Sabbath means "rest." Jewish people of Jesus' time believed that even the animals should have the day off!

Let's take a look at a present-day Sabbath.

The Jewish Sabbath (*Shabbat*) begins at sunset on Friday and ends at sunset on Saturday. All the food has to be prepared before the Sabbath starts.

On Friday evening as the sun goes down, the family welcomes the Sabbath. The women of the house light the Sabbath candles. When the candles are lit, they move their hands over them as if they were gathering up their warmth and light. They then recite a prayer of blessing.

After this, the man of the house raises a cup of wine and recites the *Kiddush*, or Sabbath grace, to give thanks for the meal. The cup is then passed around for all to share.

Find out more about what Jewish families do on the Sabbath. What do they do when they go to the Synagogue? Plan a visit to a synagogue if you can.

Remember
And Jesus obeyed his parents.

Unit 6
Jesus reveals the compassion of God

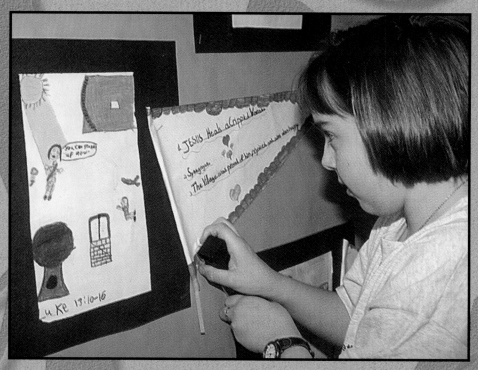

Theme 16 Jesus announces the kingdom of God
Theme 17 Jesus goes about doing good
Theme 18 They were all astounded and praised God

16 Jesus announces the kingdom of God

Juanita lay in bed in her new home in Charlottetown. She felt lonely. Everyth[ing] was so different from Guatemala, where she had lived all her ten years – until today.

Mr. and Mrs. MacDonald had adopted her. Juanita liked them but felt stran[ge] with them. They did not speak Spanish and she knew no English. Juanita wond[ered] what they were really like.

She tried to sleep, but tears kept her awak[e.] Whenever she dozed off, she remembered her mountain home near Quetzaltenango – the golden corn that grew in little plots, the sheep who bleated on the side of the steep hills, and most of all her friends Maria and Gloria.

Then she remembered the sad things. The sound of gunfire, the funeral processions, people crying. If she could only get to sleep.

In the morning Juanita's new mother drove her to school. Miss Kelly, her teacher, took her to th[e] Grade 4 classroom and introduc[ed] her. The children clapped but th[ey] seemed uncomfortable.

Juanita sat at the back of the class. She felt alone and scared.

At noon, Juanita waited until all the boys and girls had gone through the lunch line. She did not recognize any of the foods. She found an empty table and sat down by herself.

A few minutes later, Amy came over and sat beside her. She smiled and pointed to Juanita's colourful woven bracelet. Juanita pulled strands of coloured wool from her pocket and showed them to Amy.

Amy made some signs, asking Juanita if she had really made her own bracelet. Juanita smiled a big smile. Laying out the strands of wool, with Amy holding them against the table, she quickly braided a colourful bracelet. She tied the ends, made a loop and gave it to Amy.

Then something wonderful happened! Amy hugged her and took her to join some friends at their table.

Even though they couldn't speak Spanish, Juanita knew they were welcoming her. Everyone wanted one of her beautiful bracelets. And Juanita could feel their warmth.

Back in the classroom, Juanita felt alive again. She was still scared, but she belonged. She drew the bracelets she would make for her new friends, and a very special one for her new mother.

Life in Canada was looking better all the time.

(Adapted from Her Friends Gave Juanita New Life *by Janaan Manternach. Copyright NC News Service.)*

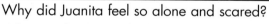

Why did Juanita feel so alone and scared?

What made Juanita feel alive again? How did she know she was being welcomed?

What kind of person do you think Amy was?

Do you know some people like Amy? How do they make others feel?

Has anything like this ever happened to you? How did you feel?

Have you ever noticed people when they were sad or lonely? What happened?

Who cares?

To be caring persons, we need to be persons who notice. We need to be able to see and hear with our hearts!

When we look through the New Testament, we see many examples of Jesus showing us how to care. He sees the short man, Zacchaeus, up in a big tree. He notices the disciples sending the children away. He hears Bartimaeus call out from the side of the road. For Jesus, the eyes and the ears are connected to the heart. And the signs of God's kingdom have to do with healing and forgiving, caring and loving.

Look in the New Testament in your Bible. How many events can you find where Jesus shows us how to care? When you finish, make a list with your friends.

Remember Jesus' Baptism. Jesus went down into the water and John baptized him in the Jordan. What happened when Jesus came out of the water? Do you remember these words?

"You are my Son, the Beloved; my favour rests on you." (Mark 1.11)

Like the gentleness of a dove, God's Spirit filled Jesus' heart with peace and strength and love.

Write this story in your own words in your remembering book. Create a title using favourite words from the story. Share it at home!

In this scene (in the synagogue in Nazareth) you can tell that Jesus is feeling strong with the power of God's Spirit. Listen to his words:

"The Spirit of the Lord is upon me,
because he has anointed me
to preach good news to the poor.
He has sent me
to proclaim release to the captives,
and recovering of sight to the blind,
to set at liberty those who are oppressed,
to proclaim the acceptable year of the Lord."
(See Luke 4.18-19.)

After hearing what Jesus proclaimed in the synagogue, what signs would the people of Nazareth look for to know that God cares for them?

List in your Big Book of Remembering all the ways Jesus said he fulfills what he read from Isaiah. Give your list this heading: "Signs of God's Kingdom" (Luke 4).

Come and see –
What we've heard,
What we've seen,
What we've touched,
Jesus Christ
the Word of life

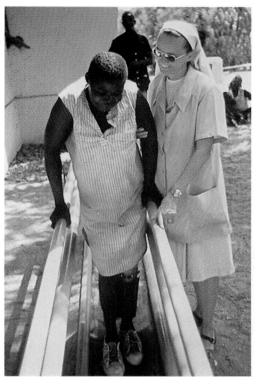

One day, Jesus' friends did not seem to understand something important that Jesus had done. Find out what Jesus said to them in Mark 8.17-21. Notice how strong Jesus' words are:

"Have you eyes that do not see, ears that do not hear?"

When John the Baptist was in prison, he sent two messengers to ask Jesus if he really is the one sent by God to save God's people. Jesus answered:

"Go back and tell John what you have seen and heard: the blind see again, the lame walk, lepers are cleansed, the deaf hear, the dead are raised to life, and the Good News is proclaimed to the poor...."

Remember

The kingdom of God is about the blind seeing, the lame walking, the deaf hearing, the dead rising and the poor hearing the good news.

Read the message for yourself in Luke 7.22.

17 Jesus goes about doing good

At work!

What is going on in these pictures?
Have you ever visited a workplace?

Tell your story of the workers and their work.

The work of hands and feet

This bulletin board is filled with scenes of Jesus going about doing God's work – touching, healing, celebrating, giving life.

Celebrating at Cana
John 2.1-12

Curing the paralytic
Mark 2.3-12

Curing the deaf man
Mark 7.31-35

Raising the widow's son
Luke 7.11-16

Curing a demoniac
Luke 4.33-36

Curing the blind man
Mark 8. 22-26

Curing the blind man
Luke 18.35

Curing the leper
Luke 5.12-14

Cure of an official's son
at Cana in Galilee
John 4.46-53

Preaching and healing
the sick
Matthew 4.23-25

Healing a woman on
the Sabbath
Luke 13.10-16

Read about these events in the Gospels
and answer these questions:

Whom did Jesus help?

How did he help them?

Why did he help them?

What did Jesus say?

Have you ever wondered about the work of your hands?

Have you ever thought about how you use them?

What signs of the kingdom do you see on the bulletin board on pages 107-108?

Make your own kingdom storyboard, cartoon strip or puppet play.

Remember

Like Jesus, we work for God's kingdom whenever we care for one another and bring peace, justice and forgiveness to our world.

18 They were all astounded and praised God

Do these headlines sound familiar?

International aid to flood victims

Monsoon rains leave thousands homeless. International organizations are rushing in with food and medicine. People from many countries are donating money, clothing and temporary shelters.

Aid from all over the world pours into a drought-stricken African country

After years without rain, thousands of people are suffering from hunger and disease. Food supplies are gone as farmlands disappear and animals die. The world community works together to bring food and medicine to the suffering people.

Canada helps war victims

Children from a war-torn country are flown to Canada for medical treatment. Canadian families are accepting these children into their homes as they await surgery. Hospitals are donating their staff and facilities to look after the medical needs of these children.

The whole community helps!

Hundreds of people come to the aid of a vacationing family. News of their lost child reaches the community Saturday morning. Within hours, the community organizes a search. Men, women and children comb the woods of a nearby park looking for the eleven-year-old. Five hours later, the boy is found. He is scared but safe. The boy's parents are overwhelmed with gratitude.

Children's Wish Foundation

Hundreds of businesses and individuals are donating money. They want to help fulfill the dreams of children who are dying from diseases such as cancer. Many kids from all across this country have been helped by the Children's Wish Foundation.

Check out newspapers and magazines. Discover how people from your community, your country and the world have responded to situations like these.

Giving praise and thanks

"...all the people were overjoyed at all the wonders he worked"
(Luke 13.17)

Go back to the bulletin board shown on pages 107 and 108. Do you remember these events? Read the stories again in the New Testament in your Bible. This time, watch for the people's reaction to Jesus. What did they say? How did they feel? What did they do?

Together with your friends, design several small flags and write down the crowd's reaction. Use these questions to help you:

What is the name of the story?

Where did it take place?

What is the crowd's reaction?

Create a litany of praise and thanks and celebrate with your friends the wonderful works of God!

new word

litany: a form of prayer in which a response is repeated between short prayers.

Remember

"A great prophet has arisen among us!" and "God has visited [God's] people!"
(Luke 7.17)

Unit 7
Jesus says, "I am the Way"

19 Jesus is sent to bring God's love

Lord,
*   we worship you.*
Keep us on our
*   Lenten journey.*
Light up our hearts
*   with Easter's*
*   bright promise.*

What do you remember about the season of Lent at home, in your parish and at school?

Did you notice anything different at church on Sunday?

Why do you think these changes were made?

What is happening in this picture? Why?

Do you know what the word "Lent" means? Turn to page 117 to find out.

The Tale of the Little River

In the heart of a great desert, Little River was searching its way through the burning sands to the Great Ocean. When the river had begun its journey, it was quick and bubbly and eager to travel. Now, as it twisted and turned among sharp rocks and hot sands, it had slowed down to a mere trickle.

One day, in the heat of the noon hour sun, it thought in its heart, "I can scarcely go on. I'm too thirsty, too hot, too weak. But I must struggle on, I must conquer these sands. I will win my way to the Great Ocean."

But as evening covered the desert in its dark shadows, the river was frightened and lonely. It was no longer sure that it was even headed in the right direction.

The Great Wind paused in its flight overhead. "Little River," she called, "why do you struggle so, night and day?"

"To reach the Great Ocean." Then Little River added weakly, "Wherever it is."

The Great Wind laid her gentle hand upon the river's shoulders. "You can get there. You will. But you must trust me to help you. Do you want me to help you, Little River?"

The river paused. It had struggled so long the only way it knew how. The Great Wind understood its fears. "Yes," she assured the river, "you will have to change. But you can get to the Great Ocean if you are willing."

"Yes." The river had decided. "I am willing to change. Will you help me, Great Wind, that I may at last make my way to the Ocean?"

The Great Wind swept down immediately, taking the moisture from the river and drawing it up high into the air. High up into the night, away above the desert floor, river droplets were carried onward. Faster and faster, the wind soared on its way to the sea. Night faded and morning came, but on the river droplets flew, held securely in the arms of the Great Wind.

Late in the morning of the new day, a sparkle was seen in the distance. "Could it be?" wondered Little River. On they flew until below them the Great Ocean rolled and surged in welcome. And now the Wind drew back – she had done her

part – and Little River swooped down into the shining depths of the waves. It plunged in among the great white squalls, cool and strong now after its desert trip. The Great Wind hovered, pleased that Little River had at last found its way.

The Great Ocean, the Great Wind, the happy Little River – together they sparkled in the noonday sun.

What role did the Great Wind play?

What did Little River decide to do?

Why was this hard to do?

What did the Great Ocean do?

How is this a story of trust?

Nicodemus goes to Jesus

It was very dark that night. Through the streets of Jerusalem, Nicodemus slipped quietly, making his way to the house where Jesus was staying.

Finish the story in your remembering book. Use John 3.1-18 in your Bible as a guide. Think about these questions as you create your story:

What kind of man do you think Nicodemus was?

How is Little River like Nicodemus?

Jesus tells Nicodemus that he must be born again of the Spirit. What does Jesus mean?

What changes do you think Nicodemus might have to make?

Would these changes be easy to make?

Draw a picture to go with your story. Take your story home to share with your family.

Construct a weathervane out of cardboard and write these words on it: "The wind blows where it wills." Hang it in a place at home where it will catch the wind.

new word

Lent: means "springtime."

Remember

In Baptism, we are born anew "of water and the Spirit."

20 Jesus is the living water

What makes water
so special?

**With your friends,
create a Water Log
by listing all the
ways we use water.**

"Give me a drink."

"He came to a city of Samaria, called Sychar, near the field that Jacob gave to his son Joseph. Jacob's well was there, and so Jesus, wearied as he was with his journey, sat down beside the well.... There came a woman of Samaria to draw water. Jesus said to her, 'Give me a drink.'"
(John 4.5-7)

Can you finish the story?

Open your Bible to the New Testament and read John 4.14.

What kind of water do you suppose Jesus was talking about when he said, "Whoever drinks of the water that I shall give ... will never thirst"?

"Come, see a man who told me all that I ever did. Can this be the Christ?"

Use clay or cardboard to mould a tabletop scene of the event in the picture.

"Everyone who drinks of this water will thirst again, but whoever drinks of the water that I shall give him will never thirst; the water that I shall give him will become in him a spring of water welling up to eternal life." (John 4.13-14)

Invite one or more persons preparing to celebrate Christian initiation at Easter to visit. Ask them all about their Lenten journey.

Remember
"Whoever drinks of the water that I shall give will never thirst." (See John 4.14.)

21 Jesus shows us the Father

The Prince's great question

The Prince could no longer bear it. Every day, he faced the same routine. His clothes were laid out for him, and someone said "Good morning, your majesty. You will wear the blue tunic this morning." A healthy breakfast was served to him to prepare him for the day's activities. "Good morning, your majesty. You will have oatmeal this morning." No one ever asked him what he wanted. It was so necessary that he be in good health that there was no choice at all. After all, what would happen to the kingdom if the Prince were to get sick, or even die?

"Your majesty, your lessons..." "Your majesty, archery practice awaits you..." "Your majesty, your presence is required in the drawing room." His majesty had had enough.

One morning, while he was practising his horsemanship, the Prince decided to take matters into his own hands. Galloping full tilt, he cleared the castle gates and headed for the distant forest. "At last," he thought to himself, "I have the freedom I have longed for. Now there is someone I must see, someone who will help me find meaning in this life I must lead."

On and on he rode, not quite sure of the direction he should take. Finally, he came to the bottom of a steep hill. Up near the top of the hill, he could barely make out the shape of a thatched hut. Tying his horse to the trunk of a nearby tree, he struggled up the slope until at last he reached his goal.

In a small patch of garden, a wise old woman bent over her carefully-tended bean plants. With great effort after his hard climb, the young Prince straightened his shoulders and called to her, "Wise woman! I have come a great distance to talk to you. Please tell me, what is the meaning of this life I must lead?"

The woman continued at her work, carefully tying the stalks around a stake and fastening them to the support. The prince waited a few moments, and feeling that the wise woman was thinking over his great question, he sat down nearby to wait for her answer. After a while, when she still had not given him the answer he was looking for, he got up and took a stake from a pile lying on the ground. Without saying a word, he pushed the stake into the soil beside the bean plant next to the one the woman was working on. "Thank you," she said simply, and began tying up the next plant. The Prince placed another stake into the ground, and another, and another, until he and the woman had worked their way down the row of beans.

Having finished the work at hand, the Prince felt sure that the woman would reward him with an answer to his question. But at just that moment, a stranger appeared at the edge of the garden. "Help me!" he gasped, and collapsed upon the ground.

The Prince and the woman rushed to the stranger and carried him inside the hut. Finding a large wound on his leg, they set about cleaning and binding it. Then the Prince ran to get a dipper of water for the wounded man to drink, so that he would regain his strength. Finally, as evening approached, the stranger began to come around and was able to sit up and speak to them. Only then did the woman and the Prince realize how hungry they were, after all their work.

"I'll go and pick some of the fresh beans that we have tended," the Prince offered. And soon he returned to the hut with a basket of beans ready for cooking. In no time at all, the three of them were happily eating the beans and talking about the day's activity.

The Prince had almost forgotten his purpose in finding the wise woman. "Wise woman," he said to her, "you still have not told me the answer to my question. How will I find meaning in this life that I must lead?"

"You have already found the answer," the woman replied. "How is it that you do not see what that answer is?"

The Prince looked confused, so the woman helped him. "Today, when you came to see me, you helped me with my garden. Then, when this man came, you tended to his need with great care. If you hadn't, if he had had to wait for attention, he might have died – you never know. And now, with your help, we have this meal to share together and to keep us going for another day. So the meaning in your life is clear: Help those around you. Help them now. In helping others, you have helped yourself."

(Inspired by Leo Tolstoy.)

Seeing with new eyes

Philip said to Jesus, "Lord, show us the Father, and we shall be satisfied."

Imagine that you are Philip. Listen to Jesus' answer.

"Have I been with you so long, and yet you do not know me, Philip? Anyone who has seen me has seen the Father. How can you say, 'Show us the Father'? Do you not believe that I am in the Father and the Father is in me? The words that I say to you I do not speak on my own authority; but the Father who dwells in me is at work. Believe me that I am in the Father and the Father in me. If you can't believe me because of my words, believe me because of my work of healing, forgiving, teaching, working signs. Trust me for what I do; it is a sign that God is here."
(See John 14.9-11.)

These Grade 4 students prepare a Lenten tree to show Jesus' work of healing, forgiving and caring.

What must Philip do to know God?

Why does Philip want to know God?

Do you think that Philip and the Prince are a little alike?

What do we mean by "seeing with new eyes"?

Have you ever wondered what God is really like?

Have you ever asked questions like "Who made God?"

Write down some of your questions. Then, share your thoughts with your friends.

> *Remember*
> "If you know me, you know my Father, too."
> (See John 14.7.)

Unit 8
Jesus gives his life for us

22 Jesus goes up to Jerusalem

"The Jewish Passover drew near, and many of the country people who had gone up to Jerusalem. . . looked out for Jesus, saying to one another as they stood about in the Temple, 'What do you think? Will he come to the festival or not?' The chief priests and Pharisees had by now given their orders: anyone who knew where he was must inform them so that they could arrest him." (See John 11.55-57.)

 Why did Jesus have enemies?

Jesus had gone about curing people and teaching and proclaiming the good news. It's hard for us to understand why some people wanted to arrest him.

Be the detective and find out! Here are two questions you need to prepare your case:
- **Did Jesus do anything wrong?**
- **Why were some people against him?**

You can find clues in the New Testament in your Bible. Read two or three of these passages:
- **Matthew 12.9-14**
- **Matthew 22.15-22**
- **Matthew 12.22-24**
- **Mark 2.1-11**
- **Matthew 13.53-58**

When you have put together your evidence, give your report.

Jesus decides

Jesus came back to Jerusalem, even though he knew that his enemies wanted to get rid of him. Perhaps he could have run away across the Jordan River to the desert. But he didn't.

Jesus went to Jerusalem because he knew he had to be faithful to his Father's message. In his heart there was a deep trust that his Father would not leave him to struggle alone.

A prayer of trust

Let us remember how Jesus was always faithful. He trusted in his Father's help. At the Last Supper, he reminded his friends to trust as well.

Leader: *Sometimes we are weak and want to give up.*
All: *WE TRUST IN YOU, LORD.*

Leader: *Sometimes we are sad and we feel all alone.*
All: *WE TRUST IN YOU, LORD.*

Leader: *Sometimes we feel like being mean to each other.*
All: *WE TRUST IN YOU, LORD.*

Leader: *Sometimes we are afraid to stand up for what is right.*
All: *WE TRUST IN YOU, LORD.*

Leader: *Sometimes our friends turn against us and laugh.*
All: *WE TRUST IN YOU, LORD.*

Leader: *Sometimes we are blamed when we do something good.*
All: *WE TRUST IN YOU, LORD.*

Remember
He suffered under Pontius Pilate.

Continue on with the litany and end with this prayer:

Loving God,
we thank you
for your Son, Jesus,
who has given us
an example of trust and faithfulness. Amen.

23 Jesus gives himself

Whenever guests came to a Jewish house, a servant or slave would welcome them and wash their feet.

When Jesus was at the house of Simon the leper, he was not welcomed in the usual way. A woman came and washed his feet, and Jesus praised her for her love and care.

At the Last Supper, Jesus showed his love and care for his disciples when he did the job of a servant. They were amazed! They did not understand his actions.

Read in the New Testament in your Bible the story of Jesus washing his disciples' feet: John 13.12-15.

How would you feel if you were Peter and Jesus wanted to wash your feet?

How do you think Peter felt after the foot-washing?

Jesus has asked us to love and serve one another. What are some ways of doing this?

At what time in the Church year does the Christian community celebrate a ritual foot-washing? Why?

The Eucharist is a "sacrifice of praise"

At the Eucharist, we remember the last meal Jesus shared with his friends. Read the story in Matthew 26.26-29. We remember especially how Jesus gave himself for others:

Blessed be Jesus, whom you sent
to be the friend of children
and of the poor.
He came to show us how we can
love you, Father, by loving
one another.
He came to take away sin, which
keeps us from being friends,
and hate, which makes us
all unhappy.

(From the *"Eucharistic Prayer for Children II"*)

Jesus' whole life was a sacrifice of praise. "Sacrifice" in this case means giving oneself to others.

We, too, ask God to help us be a living sacrifice of praise:

Lord, look upon this sacrifice which
you have given to your Church;
and by your Holy Spirit,
gather all who share this one
bread and one cup into the one
body of Christ,
a living sacrifice of praise.

(From *"Eucharist Prayer IV"*)

Can you suggest some good ways for us to praise God in our lives?

Give yourself

When Old Mrs. Hennessey
    opened the door,
Susan saw parcels and cards
    on the floor.
"It's my birthday," the old
    lady said with a smile,
"I'm here all alone. Can you
    stay for a while?"
And later while talking she
    grew very sad:
"Now this is the eightieth birthday
    I've had.
Every year I get parcels piled up
    in the hall,
But rather than parcels I'd love
    them to call.
I know you've worked hard at
    your lessons all day.
I'm sure you'd prefer to go out and
    to play.
I have beautiful cards in a line on
    the shelf
But your present was nicest –
    you gave me yourself.

Christy Kenneally

Reprinted from *Miracles and Me*.
© 1986 by Christy Keneally.
Used by permission of Paulist Press

In the poem, Mrs. Hennessey believes Susan gave herself as a present.
How can you give yourself?
How might this giving be a "sacrifice of praise"?

new word

Eucharist: thanksgiving.

Remember

Jesus has given his life for us.

131

24 Jesus dies for us

"Hosanna! Blessed is he who comes in the name of the Lord!"
(Mark 11.9)

Following the way of Jesus

During Holy Week in Jerusalem, the early Christians used to follow the route taken by Jesus as he carried his cross to Calvary. Along the way, they would pause for prayer and remember what had happened to Jesus. The places where they stopped were known as "stations." There were fourteen stations. Churches around the world put up pictures of the stations so Christians could follow the way of the cross in their own parishes.

Have you noticed the stations of the cross in your parish? Take the time to see them during the next few weeks. Make the way of the cross together.

*"Father, into your hands
I commit my spirit!"*

 What do you remember
most about making the
way of the cross with
your friends?

Can you identify these drawings of the stations of the cross?

Draw your own way of the cross and bring it home to share with your family.

Lord, by your cross and resurrection
you have set us free.
You are the Saviour of the world.

Remember
Jesus died for us
on the cross.

Unit 9
"My Lord and my God!"

Theme 25 He who was crucified is risen!
Theme 26 We have seen the Lord!
Theme 27 "Now at last they know"

25 He who was crucified is risen!

Христос Воскрес! Воістину Воскрес!

CHRIST IS RISEN!   HE IS RISEN INDEED!

Have you ever heard such good news that you just couldn't believe it? What did you do?

What do you suppose the disciples did when they heard the good news for the first time?

Can you tell a story from the picture and words on this page?

138

Brenda, Nicole, Rachelle

Early one morning
After Jesus' death
Something strange happened
The three women who had followed Jesus
Entered the tomb and saw nothing. They learned of the
Resurrection

Early in the morning
At dawn there's a
Sign of new life ~
To rejoice is our task ~
Easter is a time to remember ~ Jesus has
Risen from the dead ~
　　　　Ole Jensen & Greg Gervais

These poems show what Easter means to Brandie, Nicole, Rachelle, Ole and Greg. They are Grade 4 students like you.

What does Easter mean to you?

Pair up with a friend and create your own acrostic poem. Follow these instructions:
- **Write the word EASTER down your page.**
- **Think of sentences that describe what happened to the disciples at the empty tomb.**
- **Arrange and write the sentences so that the first word in each line starts with the right letter of the word EASTER.**
- **Lines do not have to rhyme.**

The rainbow day

September 18, 1984

Everybody in Fort Simpson was excited. For months they had been preparing for the Pope's visit, and now everything was ready: the special tent, the buckskin vestments, the warm welcome for Pope John Paul II. Many of the children were so excited that they could hardly sit still. "He'll soon be here!" they said to each other.

It was dark when the Pope left Edmonton. But as his plane drew closer to Fort Simpson, a heavy fog rolled in and smothered the entire area. It was impossible to land in such a fog! The plane circled high above Fort Simpson as the people on the ground gazed upward. They could hear the plane, but they knew that their welcome would have to wait. The plane could not land.

There was no miracle that day. The fog did not lift. Disappointed, Pope John Paul had to go back. Everyone in Fort Simpson was left to put away the memories of a visit that didn't happen.

But before the Pope left Canada, he gave something to the people who had waited for him.

Speaking to them over the radio, he promised that, with God's help, he would return to Fort Simpson and have his visit with them another time.

September 20, 1987

Three long years passed before the Pope had another chance to visit. This time, his plane was able to touch down in Fort Simpson. The morning had been a wet one, with grey clouds and plenty of rain. But as the Pope walked among the hundreds of people who had gathered to welcome him, the sun burst out and a magnificent rainbow bridged the sky.

The promise was kept!

What foods have you chosen for your Easter party?

How do you plan to welcome your guests?

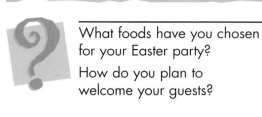

Share the story of the breakfast on the lakeshore (John 21.1-17) during your celebration. Use these questions to chat about the breakfast event:

How do you think the disciples are feeling at first? Why?

How do you think they felt when they recognized Jesus on the shore?

Jesus has bread and fish ready for the disciples to eat. In what other stories do you remember Jesus feeding people?

Remember

"Jesus was revealed to the disciples after he was raised from the dead." (John 21.14)

141

26 We have seen the Lord!

I n the evening, the disciples gathered in a room they all knew well. When they were together, they were a little happier, a little more protected from the dangers they all felt around them. So many things had happened – some were terrible things. And now there was this other news – that Jesus had risen from the dead! No one knew what would happen next.

Suddenly, Jesus was there, standing among them. "Peace be with you," he said. They all moved back as if they didn't know him. He showed them the marks in his hands and again said, "Peace be with you." He talked to them, and they knew it was really Jesus.

But where was Thomas? He was not with them as they huddled together in the room. When he arrived, they all rushed to tell him, "We have seen the Lord!"

Thomas found this hard to believe. "Unless I see the marks on his hands and feet, I won't believe what you are saying," he told them.

Several days later, when the whole group was together again, Jesus came and stood among them once more. He looked steadily at Thomas: "Put your finger into the holes in my hands," he said. "Give me your hand – put it here, into my side. Doubt no longer, but believe."

Thomas was overcome. "My Lord and my God!" he said to Jesus.

(See John 20.19-28.)

142

The eleven disciples went to Galilee, to a mountain. They found Jesus there and fell down in awe before him, although some hesitated.

(See Matthew 28.16-17.)

Use clay or modelling dough to make a model of someone showing a posture of worship or adoration. Or draw a picture in your remembering book.

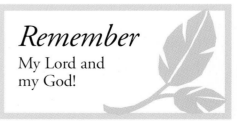

Remember

My Lord and
my God!

27 "Now at last they know"

There are many stories in the Bible about people who trust in God. These people discover that God is always with them, protecting and comforting them. Read this prayer psalm. It talks about how people like this feel.

Psalm 139

Before I was born,
you made each little part of me in secret.

While I was hidden in my mother's womb,
you watched me grow.
You saw my bones begin to form
and join together.

From the first moment of my life
you knew me!

I praise you, Lord,
and I am filled with wonder.
For everything you do
is strange and marvellous.

God the Father is never far away
– he loves us too much
to leave us all on our own.
That's why we praise him!

You know me, Lord, so very well,
you know when I get up.
You know when I go back to sleep,
you know each thing I do.

You know what I am going to say
before I even speak!
You are always close to me.
You're wonderful, O Lord.

So if I climb the highest hill,
you would be there with me.
And if I swam beneath the waves,
you'd still be there with me.

Even in the dark at night
you would be next to me.
Yes, even then I could not hide,
you would be there with me.

(From *Praise* by A.J. McCallen)

I would hide in an apple tree. *(Rita Khouri)*

Finish this sentence in your remembering book: "Even if I hid _____ you would still be there." Draw a picture of yourself in your hiding place. Do you feel God's presence there?

Jesus, too, had a special prayer to comfort his disciples before he died. He wanted them to feel safe and strong, because he would not be with them for much longer. This is how he prayed:

Father, the hour has come: I have finished the work that you gave me to do.
I have made your name known to these you have given to me.
Now at last they know that all you gave me comes indeed from you;
for I have given them the teaching you gave to me.
I pray for them because they belong to you.
Protect them and consecrate them in the truth.
May they all be one as we are one.
May the love with which you love me be in them,
*   so I may be with them.*
(See John 17.1-26.)

Take the words of this prayer home to share with your family.

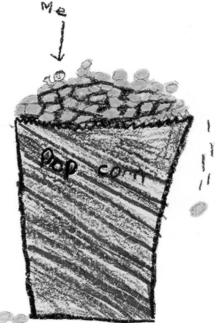

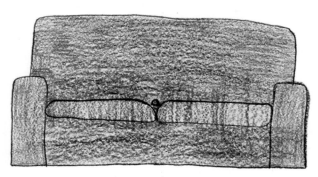

I am hiding between the pillows of the couch.
(Angie MacNeil)

I am hiding in the popcorn.
(Liam Durnin)

145

How did you celebrate your belonging to God?

What was your favourite part of the celebration? Draw a picture in your remembering book of this part.

Remember

"May they be one even as we are one." (John 17.22)

Unit 10
Jesus' Spirit is with us

Theme 28 The Holy Spirit will bring us to Jesus Christ
Theme 29 You shall be my witnesses
Theme 30 We celebrate our story: Come and See!

28 The Holy Spirit will bring us to Jesus Christ

Luke tells us about a promise that Jesus made to his followers before he returned to his Father. For forty days, he had been showing himself alive, and his friends were filled with joy. Now, as he was ready to leave them, he told them to stay in Jerusalem for what the Father had promised. That promise was the help his followers needed to continue his work: "You will receive power when the Holy Spirit comes on you, and then you will be my witnesses not only in Jerusalem but throughout Judea and Samaria, and indeed to the ends of the earth." (Acts 1.8)

What would this power from the Holy Spirit do for the disciples?

What did Jesus mean by being a "witness"?

Helped by the Holy Spirit on Pentecost, the disciples lost their fear and dared to speak openly about the truth Jesus had taught them. Here is a story about Peter, and how he spoke to the people of Jerusalem for the first time:

Peter, the fisherman. Peter, the terrified man who had denied that he even knew Jesus. This same Peter now stood before the learned and holy men of Jerusalem and shouted: "All you who live in Jerusalem, make no mistake about this. Listen carefully to what I have to say!"

And he told them about Jesus, how he had lived and died, and how God had raised him from the dead. Peter also told his listeners about the gifts of the Holy Spirit, which Jesus had promised.

"You must be baptized in the name of Jesus Christ and receive the gift of the Holy Spirit. This promise was made for you and for your children."

Many people heard what Peter was saying and were baptized. The word of Jesus was beginning to spread.

Remember

"The Holy Spirit will bring to your remembrance all that I have said to you." (John 15.26)

29 You shall be my witnesses

Who are your Easter people? Why would you call them disciples?

How did these memory people help you to know God better?

Thank you, Peter, for coming our way, you showed us that our doubts, like yours, can all be swept away.

Thank you, Nicodemus, for coming our way, you showed us that by braving the night we still might find the day.

Thank you, Nonna, for coming our way, you helped us bake the Easter bread and taught what traditions say.

Thank you, Jesus, for being with us every day, you teach us how to care for those we meet along the way.

Add your favourite memory persons to the list, showing how they helped you to know God better.

Do you remember the secret code you drew or painted on your pendant at the beginning of the year? Your code told a story about you – who you are and what things you treasure.

The early Christians also had a code like yours. It was kept secret because they had many enemies who wanted to stamp out the new religion that was spreading so quickly. That secret code is known as the Apostles' Creed.

The Apostles' Creed

I believe in God, the Father almighty, creator of heaven and earth.
I believe in Jesus Christ, his only Son, our Lord.
He was conceived by the power of the Holy Spirit
   and born of the Virgin Mary.
He suffered under Pontius Pilate,
   was crucified, died, and was buried.
He descended to the dead.
On the third day he rose again.
He ascended into heaven,
   and is seated at the right hand of the Father.
He will come again to judge the living and the dead.

I believe in the Holy Spirit,
   the holy catholic Church,
   the communion of saints,
   the forgiveness of sins,
   the resurrection of the body,
   and the life everlasting.

Living as Jesus' disciples

By sharing
our time…

By including
everyone…

By forgiving those who
have hurt us…

By offering to help…

By visiting people who are sick or people with disabilities…

Do you believe in
   God the Father?

Yes, we believe.

Do you believe in
   God the Son?

Yes, we believe.

Do you believe in
   God the Spirit?

Yes, we believe.

We believe in God;
   yes, we believe.

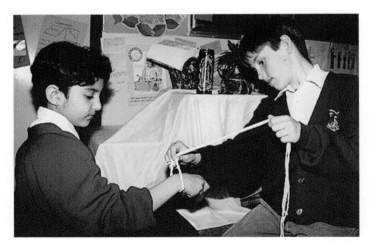

Remember

"As you did it to
one of the least…,
you did it
to me."
(Matthew
25.40)

30 We celebrate our story Come and See!

A stump is a bundle of stories

When we walk in the woods we pass stumps and rarely pause to look. Trees filled with life and fruit catch our attention. Yet, when we do take the time to sit on a stump our imaginations run wild. We imagine what that stump once was: a tree filled with life and fullness that pushed its roots deep into the soil and its leaves out to sun, wind and rain. Often when we explore a stump we find little shoots, alive and green, springing from it. This stump may have a future yet! A stump holds inside it a past, a present and a possible future.

Big Blossom

It was a chilly day in Apple Hill Park where sweet apples was all you could smell. There were Pine trees, Maple trees and Oak trees but most of all Apple trees. The largest Apple tree who they called the Big Blossom made the freshest, juiciest and sweetest apples ever. They depended on the Big Blossom every year to win the award for the best apples.

It was apple picking season but farmer Joe the owner of the Big Blossom thought (well he knew) that they wouldn't get to pick any apples this year because they weren't yet ripened and tomorrow they were expecting 20 cm of early snow. Oh well, it will melt, farmer Joe thought. There's always next year. He went to bed not covering or sheltering the tree in any

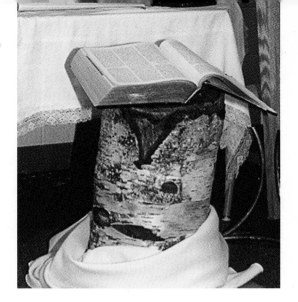

way. The weather changed to a blizzard, almost a meter of snow. Cozy in bed, farmer Joe didn't have a clue about what was happening to the Big Blossom. Frozen with no warmth or food, the Big Blossom's apples were falling off one by one. Just then the snow turned to hail and suddenly a chunk of hail hit the frozen tree and CRACK! the top of the Big Blossom fell and with a gust of wind, blew away.

In the morning farmer Joe peered out the window and said "HOLY SMOKES!" He ran outside in his bathrobe and then he ran to Apple Hill Park. "NO!" he screamed. "My tree!" Well, farmer Joe's town no longer won the award for the best apples ever and Apple Hill Park no longer smelled like sweet apples, but for many generations children have sat and played on the stump not knowing its great history. So if you ever visit Apple Hill Park, make sure you see the stump.

Emily

The Forgotten Stump

Once upon a time, there lived a willow tree in a beautiful, green forest. One night there was an awful storm. It came on so suddenly that it almost blew off people's rooftops. It roared with lightning and thunder. The leaves and branches on the poor willow tree crashed to the ground like hailstones while the wind roared with anger!!! All the animals raced for their homes in the forest. Trees fell by the hundreds. The willow tree was very frightened and could not wait until the terrible storm was over.

Afterwards, when it was calm and peaceful again, the willow tree watched and waited for hours, hoping that the animals of the forest would return to live there once again. For quite a few days the willow tree did not dare to sway his branches in the wind. He just stood there helplessly, until one day a lumberjack came into the woods. Suddenly, the willow tree knew that the lumberjack was coming closer and that this was going to be the end of him. With a few mighty chops of the axe, the beautiful willow tree was cut down till all that remained was a small stump. The little stump was heartbroken and to make things worse, the chatter of the animals and the singing of the birds had faded away. The spirit of the forest had passed

157

away. The little stump felt abandoned and alone.

However, one bright spot in its day was when Jimmie, the little blond haired, blue eyed boy from down the road came after school to visit. He would sit on the stump drawing pictures and writing poetry and he would talk about his thoughts and feelings to the lonely little stump.

One day Jimmie did not come. It went on like that for a few days, then weeks, then months. Jimmie had found new interests and forgotten all about the little stump. Once again the small stump felt sad and alone. All winter long it sat cold and forgotten.

But one beautiful day spring arrived and there was excitement in the air. Animal families and their new babies, and all the birds finally returned home, and brought back life and spirit to the forest. The little stump felt happy and relieved

because once again he had become a home for the rabbits, squirrels and birds. Even Jimmie came by to visit once in a while. The little stump was very grateful and would never be lonely again.

The End

Katie

I'm a Tree!

Good Morning! My name is Laura Leaves. I am a maple tree that stands in front of an elegant church. I am admired by a Grade 4/5 teacher. Her name is Mrs. Carrol.

When I was about ten I had my first bird nest. Now I feel lose-leafed because I was pruned not too long ago. I miss the cool summer days when people all over Ottawa would have picnics under my shady branches. I'm hopeful about being climbed by the junior kids. I am planning to make friends with a tree not far away.

Luba

My life story

Hi! My name is Sammy Saw Dust. I am an old and short tree. I am standing on a church lawn that is covered with snow. Right now I am pretty sad because I just lost all my leafy hair and I have no more people friends taking my picture. I miss my young days when I had a lot of attention. I just can't wait until next spring when my leaves come back. Right now I feel weird because my friend Barky Birch just got cut down. Usually I don't get lonely because just about everyday I get visitors from the church. My favourite thing is when I hear the people sing and shivers run through my arms. I hope the next time we meet is not in your fireplace.

Alex

The 4T Story Tree

We went for a walk, and we saw a tree
On that tree we saw a bee
Beside that bee there was a flea
Together they were drinking tea

As they drank their tea with glee
They asked each other, "What do you see?"
The sky, the stars, the sun, the stream
They both agreed they loved this tree

Courtney

Remember

Let us proclaim the
mystery of faith:
Christ has died,
Christ is risen,
Christ will
come again.

Come and See, Student Book, is a catechetical program of the *Born of the Spirit* © series, developed by the National Office of Religious Education of the Canadian Conference of Catholic Bishops, Ottawa, Canada.

Approved by The Episcopal Commission for Christian Education, Canadian Conference of Catholic Bishops

Project Specialist, Child Portfolio
Myrtle Power

Editing and Writing Specialist
Anne Louise Mahoney

Year 4 Consultants
We acknowledge with gratitude the artwork, stories and photographs from Peggy Henderson, Stephanie Tomicic, Bill Marrevee and the families and children at St. Mark's Parish, Aylmer, Quebec; and from the following teachers and their Grade 4 classes: Lyla Carroll, St. George's School, Ottawa, ON; Judy Der, St. Mary's School, Vancouver, BC; Maria Domke, St. Bonaventure School, Edmonton, AB; Gail Irvine, St. Patrick's School, Victoria, BC; Beverly Laping, St. Charles Academy, Winnipeg, MB; Liz Murphy, St. Elizabeth Ann Seton School, Nepean, ON; Susan Odishaw, St. Gregory School, Regina, SK; Laurie Ruhr, St. Francis School, Regina, SK; Louise Turcotte, Holy Spirit School, Stittsville, ON.

Special thanks to all other contributors in the field, especially Ashley Barnes, Mary Boucher, Shirley Berman, Robert Bredin, Patrick Card, Mary Collis, Wanda Conway, Adrienne Corti, Margaret Craddock, Gerard Davis, Karen Doyle, Herman Falke, Doreen Kostynuik, Don MacLellan, Ken Merk, Patricia O'Conner, Diane Pellerin, Corey Tomicic.

Acknowledgements
The Scripture quotations contained herein are from the Revised Standard Version of the Bible, copyrighted 1946, 1952, 1971 by the Division of Christian Education of the National Council of the Churches of Christ in the United States of America, and are used by permission. All rights reserved.

Excerpts from the *Catechism of the Catholic Church*, Copyright © Concacan Inc. - LIBRERIA EDITRICE VATICANA, 1994, for the English translation in Canada.

Excerpts from the English translation of *The Roman Missal* © 1973, International Committee on English in the Liturgy, Inc. (ICEL); excerpts from the English translation of *Eucharistic Prayers for Masses with Children* © 1975, 1980, ICEL. All rights reserved. Used with permission.

The English translation of the Lord's Prayer, The Apostles' Creed prepared by English Language Liturgical Consultation (ELLC), 1988.

Grandma's Bread excerpts adapted from the video *Grandma's Bread*, copyright 1985 by Franciscan Communications. Reprinted by permission of St. Anthony Messenger Press/Franciscan Communications, 1615 Republic Street, Cincinnati, Ohio 45210 USA. All rights reserved.

"When Simeon First Saw Mary's Child" from *Live, Learn and Worship* (CIO Publishing), is copyrighted © 1979 by The Wadderton Group and is produced by permission.

Mother Teresa by Mary Craig, Copyright © Evans Brothers Limited, 2A Portman Mansions, Chiltern Street, London, W1M 1LE, England. All rights reserved. Used by permission.

Praise, poem based on Psalm 138 by A.J. McCallen, Copyright © HarperCollins *Publishers* Limited. All rights reserved. Used by permission.

Her Friends Gave Juanita New Life by Janaan Manternach, © Janaan Manternach. All rights reserved. Used by permission.

Basque Sheepherder and the Shepherd's Psalm by James K. Wallace from *The National Wool Grower*, Dec. 1949. Reprinted with permission of the National Wool Growers Association and the American Sheep Industry. All rights reserved.

"Give Yourself" reprinted from *Miracles and Me* by Christy Kenneally, © 1986 by Christy Kenneally. Used by permission of Paulist Press.

Art & Design
Creative Art & Design, Publications Service

Cover
Mike Pinder – photograph
Ron Tourangeau – digital imaging

Photographs
Photographs & children's art work come from pilot classes and parishes across Canada except for the following:

Berkeley Studios/United Church of Canada – 130; Robert Bredin – 6, 7, 18L, 20, 42, 50, 62, 79, 99, 112, 125, 136, 152; Elaine Brière – 149T; Skip Brooks – 132; By permission of the British Library – 37 (codex); Lyla Carroll – 94BR; CCCB/Harpell – 5, 12B, 18T, 21T, 53, 66, 68B, 69, 70, 71, 72BR, 73, 76B, 77, 78T, L, 89, 90B, 91, 113, 114, 121B, 124, 127, 134, 137-139, 142, 146, 150, 151; Terry Cherwick – 14B; Dorothy Chocolate, Native Press – 140; Adrienne Corti – 80, 86, 95B; Courtesy of Corel Corporation – 58, 81, 98, 133; Courtesy of Niagara Falls Art Gallery – "Passion of Christ"

by Wm. Kurelek – 143; Gerard Davis – 147; Herman Falke/artist – 138, 142; Joyce Harpell – 48; Richard Henderson – 72; Tom Hocker – 14T, C; Kal Husseini – 78BR; "Image Copyright" © 1996 PhotoDisc, Inc." – 85T; Doreen Kostynuik – 141B, 156; Terry Lozynsky – 75, 94TL; Magnum Photos, Inc/Micha Bar'Am – 97T; Missionary Oblates of Mary Immaculate – 105; Liz Murphy – 10T, L; National Gallery of Canada, Ottawa – "Presentation in the Temple" by John Opie – 88; Ottawa Jewish Historical Society Archives: Retrieval Search & Research – 83L, 96; Mike Pinder – 19, 118; Kevin Ryall – 95T, 84T; SKJOLD – 29B, 72T, 94BL, 102, 106T, BL, 109; Maureen Synyard – 158; Lu Taskey – 22; The Toronto Star/M. Slaughter 44T / B. Spremo – 44B; Ron Tourangeau – 16T; William van den Hengel – 82, 83R, 84, 85B; Bill Wittman – 24, 29C, 47, 57, 97B, 106BR, 121T, 149L, R.

Pottery Jars, Qumran; Isaiah Scroll (Dead Sea Scrolls), © The Israel Museum. Reproduced with permission.

Stations of the Cross from *The Footsteps of Christ* (set of 16 full colour posters), Copyright: The Olivetan Benedictine Sisters, published by McCrimmon Publishing Co. Ltd., Great Wakering, Southend-on-Sea, Essex SS3 0EQ. Used with permission.

Illustrations Nora Brown
Andrea Rasmussen – 80
Ron Tourangeau – end pages

Printed and bound in Canada by
Friesens Corporation

Published by
Publications Service, Canadian Conference of Catholic Bishops, 90 Parent Avenue, Ottawa, Ontario, Canada K1N 7B1

ISBN 0-88997-357-1

Legal Deposit National Library of Canada, Ottawa, Ontario